AF593488

MAGICIANS, WIZARDS, & SORCERERS

THE WEIRD AND HORRIBLE LIBRARY

MAGICIANS, WIZARDS, & SORCERERS

by Daniel Cohen

J. M. Dent & Sons Ltd London

First published in Great Britain 1977

Originally published in the United States of America
by J. B. Lippincott Company

Printed in Great Britain by
Butler & Tanner Ltd, Frome and London for
J. M. Dent & Sons Limited
Aldine House Albemarle Street London

ISBN 0 460 06813 X

British Library Cataloguing in Publication Data

Cohen, Daniel
Magicians, wizards and sorcerers.—(The weird and horrible library).
1. Magicians—Juvenile literature
I. Title II. Series
133.4′092′2 BF1589

ISBN 0-460-06813-X

IN MEMORY OF PUNCH

CONTENTS

MAGICIANS, WIZARDS, & SORCERERS

1
THE SECRET OF THE PYRAMIDS

MAGIC, say many of those who believe in it, is the science or art of the Magi, the priests of ancient Persia. Where the Magi learned their magic no one could say for sure, but according to tradition the knowledge could be traced back to the dawn of human civilization. Some say that the magical secrets were first revealed to the sages of Ancient Egypt. Others hold that magic has been handed down from great civilizations that were far older than Egypt. All traces of such civilizations, like Atlantis, Lemuria, and Mu, have long since disappeared.

Whatever the origins of magic, say the legends, the knowledge gave the Magi the power to rule the world. Their rule was a wise and benevolent one, but man is an imperfect being and the Magi were ultimately overthrown by the warriors. The Magi realized that mankind was not yet ready for the knowledge that they possessed, so they withdrew from public view. They hid themselves so well that people began to doubt that they had even existed. In order that the great secrets of magic should not be lost to mankind forever, the Magi carefully initiated into their number a few select and worthy individuals every generation. Thus the traditions and secrets of the ancient brotherhood could be preserved until such time as they would be revealed to the world once again.

Iamblichus was a Greek philosopher who lived in Egypt during the first half of the fourth century A.D. He is believed to have left an account of the initiation of a new member into the ancient brotherhood of the Magi during his own time.

The great sphinx of Giza, says Iamblichus, contained the entrance to the sacred passages and chambers in which the Magi held their initiation tests. A massive door was located between the forelegs of the statue. The door could be opened only by a hidden spring, the location of which was known exclusively to members of the brotherhood. A maze of corridors connected the sphinx with the chambers built beneath the Great Pyramid itself. But these corridors were so skillfully constructed that anyone who tried to go from the sphinx to the Great Pyramid without a guide was inevitably brought back by the mysterious network to the very place where he had started.

According to Iamblichus's description the postulant or candidate for admission was led blindfolded through the corridors by two Thosmothetes or guardians of the sacred rites. During the journey he was suddenly stopped, and told that he was standing at the edge of a precipice, and that if he took one more step he would fall to the bottom of a deep moat. "This abyss," said the Thosmothetes, "surrounds the Temple of the Mysteries and protects it against the temerity and curiosity of the profane. We have arrived a little too soon; our brethren have not yet lowered the drawbridge by which the initiates communicate with the sacred place. Let us wait for their arrival. But if you value your life, do not move, cross your hands on your breast and do not take off your bandage until the signal." There was no abyss, but the blindfolded and awestruck postulant could not know that.

After a few moments the postulant was again led forward, and quite suddenly the bandage was torn from his eyes. Directly in front of him a trapdoor had opened with a deafening roar, and a mechani-

The Great Sphinx and the Great Pyramid.

cal specter brandishing a scythe rose from it. "Woe to him who comes to disturb the peace of the dead," cried the specter, and the blade of the scythe brushed the postulant's head seven times. If the postulant recoiled backward, or in any other way showed fear, he had failed. The blindfold was put back over his eyes and he was led out. He could never again reapply for admission to the Sacred College of the Magi. If he passed the test he went on to further and more difficult tests.

The test with the specter was to see if the postulant could overcome the fear of death. The next test was to see if he could master the solitude of the tomb. The candidate was made to crawl through tiny dark tunnels for hours. They grew narrower and narrower until finally, when he had barely enough space in which to move at all, the tunnel opened into a large chamber. There the postulant was confronted with an oily pool of unknown depth. Behind him a curtain of flames sprang up. He plunged into the pool, not knowing whether he would drown, but found that it was just shallow enough for him to walk to the other side. Now he was in front of a huge bronze door, decorated with the carved heads of lions and other fierce beasts. The fire was extinguished, and in the blackness a voice cried out, "If you stop, you will perish. Behind you is death; before you salvation."

The exhausted and terrified postulant tried to find some way of opening the door. He pulled a brass ring, but instead of the door in front of him opening, a trapdoor opened beneath his feet and he was suspended over a gaping pit. Unknown to the postulant his fall would be broken by hidden nets, but if he let go of the ring he would have failed the test. If the postulant held the ring till the trapdoor closed he was then led into the vault beneath the Great Pyramid and was able to confront the Hierophant—keeper of the Sacred Word and head of the College of the Magi. The Hierophant's chamber was decorated with symbolic paintings which contained all of the world's magical knowledge. But these paintings could be read only by those who knew the key to the mysterious symbols.

The Hierophant was seated upon a silver throne. He wore a purple cloak, and on his forehead was a circlet of gold decorated with seven stars. Around him sat the other Magi, wearing robes of white and circlets of plain gold.

"Son of Earth," cried the Hierophant, "the men of your country believed you to be learned and wise, and you felt within yourself even greater pride than was deserved by their admiration. One day you heard that we possess a store of supernatural knowledge, and you knew no rest until you received permission to enter among us." The postulant was then made to swear on pain of a thousand horrible deaths not to reveal a single detail of what he had seen.

"Beware!" said the Hierophant. "If you have sworn only with your lips, know that we can read into your heart; and falsehood in our world is punished by death!"

The chamber was then suddenly filled with the sounds of explosions and thick smoke. When the air cleared the postulant found all the Magi standing over him with drawn swords pointing at his heart. The Hierophant reminded the postulant that he had sworn absolute obedience, and to break his oath was a double crime. The Magi then lowered their swords, and two golden goblets were brought out.

"You see these goblets?" continued the Hierophant. "The contents of one are harmless: in the other there is a violent poison. I command you to seize, without reflection, one of them—and empty it at a single draught."

If the frightened postulant hesitated or refused, four officers of the Magi known as Néocores rushed forward, threw a black veil over him, rolled him up in it and carried him away. At this point the candidate for admission knew too much to simply be returned to the world. He was imprisoned in a cellar beneath the pyramid for seven months. Each day two silent visitors brought him a ration of bread and water. For diversion he was given a book written by one of the ancient sages, on man's duty toward his fellow creatures, toward himself, and toward the Supreme Being. After the period of imprisonment the goblet test was again offered. If he failed again he was cast back into the dungeon for another seven months and the test was tried again, and so on until the test was passed or the postulant died.

While a postulant who had once failed the test could be admitted into the secret order, he could never aspire to high rank. Only those who unhesitatingly grasped one of the goblets and drank it down on the first offering might be deemed worthy of advancement in the order. After the ordeal of the goblets had been courageously faced, the Hierophant explained there had really been no danger, for both goblets contained pure wine with a little myrrh added to impart a slight bitterness.

With this disclosure, the tests seemed over. The postulant was led to a luxurious bedroom where servants removed his torn and soaking clothes, massaged him with perfumed oils, and gave him a fine robe. A magnificent meal was served to him. Afterward the curtains in his room parted, revealing a gallery of beautiful dancing girls. They surrounded the postulant and wound him in a chain made from roses.

Unknown to the postulant this was the only moment during the entire initiation when his life was in immediate, mortal danger. All the other tests, the pit, the furnace, the specter, and wine, had been tricks. But if he made so much as a move toward any of the girls, and thus profaned the purity of the mysteries, a Néocore who had glided unnoticed behind him would strike him dead.

If this subtle but dangerous test was passed the postulant was raised to the rank of Zealot, and again brought before the Hierophant who explained, "Magic is composed of two elements, knowledge and strength. Without knowledge, no strength can be complete; without some sort of strength, no one can rise in the slightest degree in the world of knowledge. Learn how to suffer, that you may become impassive; learn how to die, that you may become immortal; learn how to restrain yourself, that you may be worthy of obtaining your desire; these are the first three secrets of the new life into which we have initiated you by ordeal. Every Magus [magician] is called to become the priest of Truth, that is, the confidant of its mysteries and the possessor of its strength."

The Hierophant went on to explain how initiates into the brotherhood of the Magi could attain the power of theurgy, the power to create "works similar to those of God, by the progressive discovery of the secrets of universal life." This took seven more years of study, plus examination in "all branches of knowledge accessible to man."

The Hierophant ended his speech by warning of the danger of breaking the oath of secrecy. The new member of the brotherhood was then given a practical demonstration of what happens to perjurers.

"At the foot of the altar a brazen trapdoor was now lowered over a pit whence came the noise of rattling chains and struggle, followed by the roars of a beast and the cry of a human voice in dreadful agony, then . . . nothing: only the cold stillness of a sepulchre. 'Thus do perjurers meet their end,' said the Magi.

" 'Justice is done,' goes on the Hierophant, turning to the neophyte. 'Come observe its handiwork.' "

Upon descending into the narrow pit the neophyte saw a living sphinx tearing up a human body. The sight was so ghastly that he fainted. But this spectacle, too, was a trick using a mechanical sphinx and an artificial victim. "It was the last act of the drama of initiation and was followed by a religious banquet."

What were the secrets possessed by the ancient brotherhood? This the chronicle of Iamblichus does not reveal. Either he did not know, or he knew too well the fate of those who betrayed the brotherhood.

Today, there is no evidence of underground chambers and passages in the great sphinx or the Great Pyramid. The Magi certainly existed, but there is no real proof that they possessed magical secrets or engaged in any such fantastic rituals as described here. There is indeed no solid evidence that magical secrets of any kind really exist.

Historians may laugh at the idea that magic is a body of secret knowledge held by an ancient brotherhood. Scientists reject the theory. If the magicians exist, they say, let them show themselves and perform their magic out in the open. But the believer would reply that the lack of proof itself is proof of how well the Magi have hidden their great secrets.

Whether you accept the idea of magic or not is of little importance here. Throughout the centuries thousands of people have believed in

"Upon descending into the narrow pit the neophyte saw a living sphinx tearing up a human body."

Group of Persian Magi repenting their sorceries to a Christian saint.

it. In the pages that follow we are going to look at the lives and deeds of some of those who believed, or at least claimed, that they were following in the footsteps of the Magi; that they possessed the ancient secrets known only to a few, and that by the possession of these secrets they had become like gods.

We could not possibly hope to discuss all the magicians, wizards, and sorcerers of history in a single book or even in an encyclopedia. We have chosen some of the most famous, or notorious, representatives from ancient times to the present day. Some of the figures that we are going to discuss may in reality have had little or nothing to do with the study of magic. Some may not even have existed. But all had the reputation of possessing magical powers—and in the history of magic that is enough. In the story of the initiation into the Magi, we saw how many of the wonders of the Magi were simply tricks, illusions. In the magician's world, the line between illusion and reality, fantasy and fact, is never clear. In magic what one believes is true may be more important than what really is true.

Perhaps the magician called Simon Magus never really did fly through the air as many said he did. Perhaps he never even existed. But for nearly two thousand years Christians have damned Simon as the evil magician of the Bible, and he has profoundly influenced the Christian view of magic and magicians.

Magic, like science, has a vocabulary all its own. A *magician* may be a follower of the Magi and one who deals with all manner of supernatural events. A *wizard* is traditionally a kindly practitioner of magic, whereas a *sorcerer,* who deals mainly with spirits, is more often thought of as evil. But in practice these terms, and many others—necromancer, thaumaturge, enchanter, cunning man, even witch—can be used interchangeably.

As we have said, this tale of the ancient Magi would be rejected out of hand by scientists and scholars. Before we can properly explore the lives of history's magicians, wizards, and sorcerers, we must know what the world of science and scholarship has had to say about the history of magic.

2
THE MAGICIAN'S WORLD

EVEN THE MOST HARDENED SKEPTIC must admit that magic cannot be brushed aside as either a joke or an illusion. Belief in magic is far older than science, and far more widespread than any religion. It has survived in all parts of the world for untold centuries.

The early Christians thought that their religion would wipe the pagan belief in magic off the face of the earth. They were wrong. Magic changed, but it did not disappear.

Two hundred years ago scientists were convinced that the growth of scientific knowledge would destroy all remaining belief in magic. Science did weaken the hold of magic upon men's minds, but magic certainly did not disappear.

Right now—today—people are more interested in magic than they have been for a long time. Why? Nonbelievers can offer no single or simple answer to that question except to say that a belief in magic seems to fill some deep emotional need.

Scientists who study the behavior of animals speculate that they have been able to discern the beginnings of magical rituals among some animals. Chimpanzees, for example, hoot loudly and dash about during severe rainstorms. Chimps don't like getting wet, and perhaps they are trying to drive away the rain. More likely, however, they simply feel uncomfortable and have to "do something." Perhaps our own prehuman ancestors reacted much the same way.

Thus, say the skeptics, one reason for the ancient and universal belief in, and use of, magic may lie in our own innate behavior. When faced with a situation over which we have no control we "do something," sing, shout, dance—in order to relieve the tension. Gradually, as man's brain grew larger and stronger he began to think about what he was doing. He assumed that his ritual might have some effect upon the circumstances that he faced. The moment that thought entered primitive man's head he stopped just reacting as the apes before him had done, and he started trying to make his ritual more effective. The ritual was no longer just a biological response, it was magic.

Magic is the most self-centered of all human beliefs. To the believer everything in the universe—the stones, the plants, the stars—is somehow connected with man and his desires, his fears, his health, and even the way he looks. The universe is in turn a reflection of man. Winds become angry, rivers are hungry, and a reddish cast to the sky means it is covered with blood.

In the 1920's Sir James G. Frazer, an English scholar, produced a massive study of magic throughout human history. He contended that all primitive magic was based upon the belief in "sympathetic" relations between unrelated things. He broke down the general heading of sympathetic magic into two branches. The first was called homeopathic or imitative magic. A very early example of this type of magic is the drawings that were made by the cave men. It appears that these drawings, deep inside of caves where few could see them, served a magical rather than a decorative purpose. Some of the drawings show animals pierced by spears or caught in traps. Perhaps the animals that were caught in the pictures would also be caught in the real hunt. Some of the drawings show the animals without ears. Perhaps this was meant to magically deprive the animals of their hearing so that they could not detect the hunters sneaking up on them.

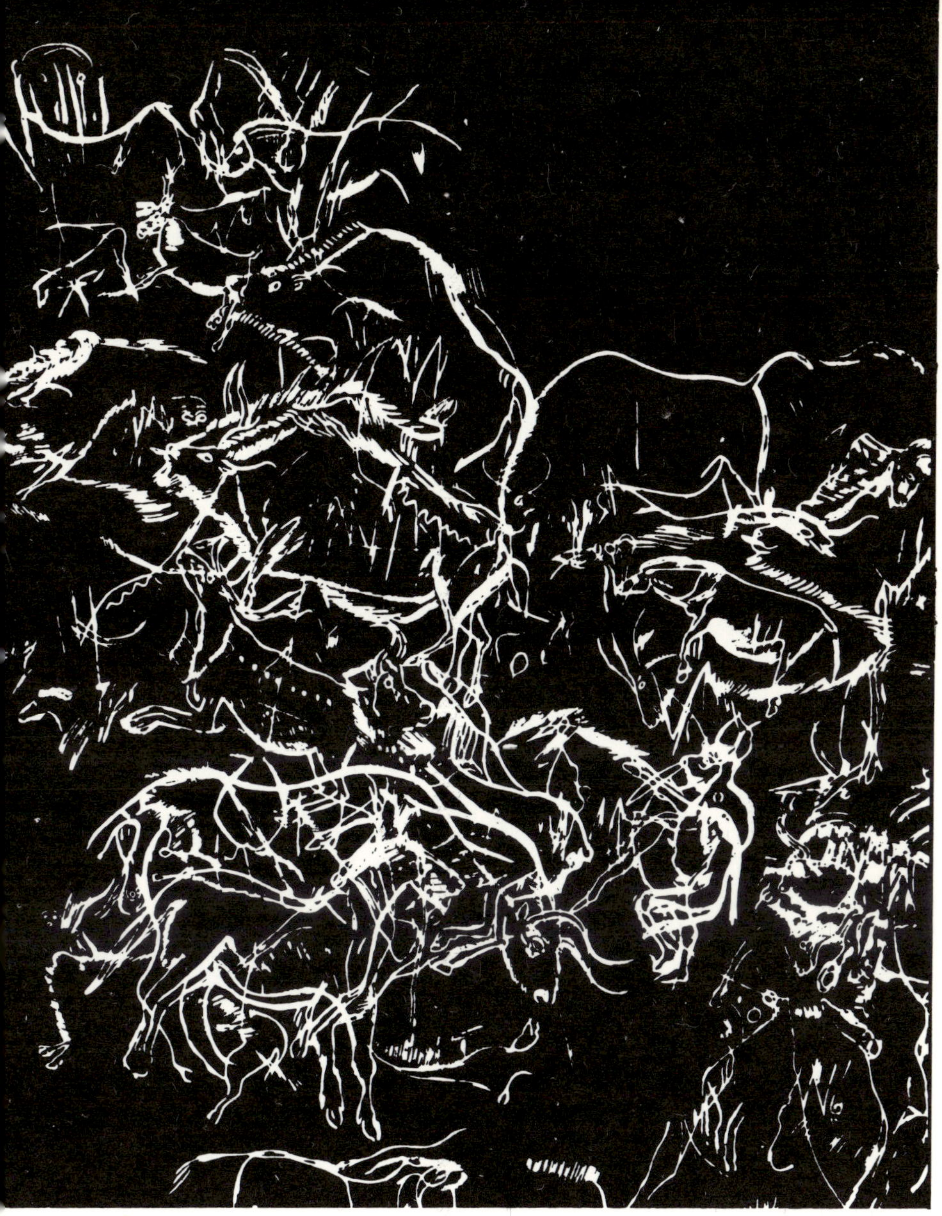

Prehistoric drawings of animals found in a French cave. In the midst of the animals is a man disguised as an animal. Scientists believe him to be a prehistoric magician.

A more familiar and more modern use of imitative magic is the so-called voodoo doll. The voodoo doctor or *houngan* makes an image of a person and sticks pins into it. The person whose image is being pierced is supposed to feel pain in corresponding places. This particular type of image magic is by no means limited to Haitian voodoo. It was widely practiced throughout the world and was popular in Europe just a few hundred years ago.

The second great branch of sympathetic magic, according to Frazer, is contagious magic. This sprang from the belief that things that had once been in contact with one another continued to influence each other after the contact has been broken. The Ewe tribe of West Africa pierces the tracks of game with a pointed stick hoping magically to "pin down" the animal that made the tracks.

Many primitive peoples believed that there was a relationship between a wounded man and the object that wounded him. Whatever was done to the wounding object would have some effect upon the wounded man. Frazer reported how in some South Pacific islands a wounded man's friends would try to get the arrow that wounded him and then keep it in a damp cool place in the belief that the inflammation of the wound would then subside. His enemies, on the other hand, would try to get hold of the arrowhead, and throw it in a fire, in the belief that this would further inflame the wound.

This particular belief has been astonishingly persistent. In England just three hundred years ago there was a serious scientific controversy concerning the "weapon salve." Many educated people thought that you could treat a wound by treating the weapon that made the wound. By plunging the weapon into a special ointment, it was argued, one could assist the "vital spirits" within the victim's body to reunite. The treatment was supposed to be good over a distance of thirty miles. According to Sir Kenelm Digby who wrote a very popular book on the subject, the weapon salve cure could be accomplished "naturally and without any magic." The treatment was still being used as a part of English folk medicine in the nineteenth century.

The principle of contagious magic can be applied to nonphysical as well as physical attributes. In the world of magic a man's name is as much a part of him as his hand. Among many primitive peoples a person's "true" name is never revealed. The fear is that some evil sorcerer will discover the name and gain magical power over that individual. Occasionally a name is so secret that the person himself does not even know it. His mother whispers a name into his ear shortly after he is born, then never speaks that name again.

The names of the dead are also powerful magical tools. Calling out a dead man's name may bring back his spirit, and since most peoples have feared the spirits of the dead this was considered evil. On the other hand it might give that spirit strength in the next world, and that was a good thing.

The names of the gods naturally possessed great supernatural powers. There is an old Egyptian legend which describes how the goddess Isis tried to capture the power of the sun god Ra and reign supreme over all the world. To do this she had to discover his secret name. Ra was so old that he dribbled and slobbered. Isis collected some of his spittle (which magically retained its connection with his body) and mixed it with earth to produce a poisonous snake. The snake stung Ra. The god was in great agony and no remedy could cure him. Finally Ra agreed that Isis could take his name if she would cure him. "I consent that Isis shall search into me and that my name shall pass from me into her." When she took Ra's name Isis really took his identity and power, according to the legend.

Frazer's two magical principles are often used to reinforce one another. The voodoo doctor who makes an image of his intended victim also tries to get a scrap of the victim's clothes to dress the doll in, or to obtain hair or nail cuttings, to stuff inside the doll. The voodoo doctor also fixes an image of the intended victim in his mind and repeats his name over and over again while thrusting in the pins.

Basic to magic is a belief that the universe is somehow alive. Men and animals have their own spirits, but so do trees, rocks, rivers, the earth, the stars, the wind—practically anything you can think of. All of these spirits can be bribed, threatened, tricked, forced, or otherwise interfered with by the proper magical means. This view of the world is called animistic, and it has been held by most people at most times.

A primary difference between magic and religion is that the religious person acknowledges the existence of a superior power—a single god, or a group of gods. This power may be appealed to but it cannot be reliably controlled. A prayer and a spell are not the same. The distinction between magic and religion is not always clear, however, and often it depends upon who is doing the classifying as to whether a belief is to be regarded as religious or magical. The early Christians accused the pagans, and their own heretical opponents, of practicing magic. The early Protestants insisted that the Roman Catholic church was full of superstitious magical rituals. The rationalists of the eighteenth century hurtled the same charges at Protestant and Catholic alike.

Even those who do not believe in the power of magic acknowledge that no system that has lasted for so many centuries can be entirely without foundation. People are just not that stupid. In a prescientific era, there was no reason for not believing in magic. The African tribesman or medieval peasant who was struck with a serious disease had no modern medical treatment to cure his ailment. All he could do was call upon the tribal witch doctor or the village wizard to perform his magic. If the sick man recovered, everyone hailed the strong magic of the witch doctor or wizard. If the patient died people assumed that the evil spirits were too strong.

Often it is hard to determine just what course of action is really magical. For several hundred years the educated physicians of Europe treated their patients by bleeding and purging them in order to restore the balance of the "four humors" of their bodies. We now know that the theory of the humors of the body was entirely false. The drastic treatment the physicians administered probably killed many people who would otherwise have recovered. Any sick man was better off with a superstitious magican who used spells and charms and at least didn't weaken his patient or inflict any unnecessary suffering upon him. Who was more magical, the learned physician and his educated patient or the illiterate wizard and his equally ignorant patient?

Another reason for believing in magic is that often magic does "work" simply because people believe strongly enough in it. Modern psychologists know that what a person thinks or believes strongly affects the way he feels. In past ages men knew nothing of psychology. All they knew was that if a sorcerer put a curse on them they felt sick. Even in modern times there are well-documented cases in which a person who believed that he had been hexed or bewitched actually sickened and died. The real power of this sort of magic does not lie in anything the magician does, but in the belief of the victim. The voodoo doctor will not hide his doll, rather he will put it where the intended victim is sure to see it, so that he knows that he has been hexed. The spell will have no effect upon the person who truly regards all magic as nonsense.

In the same way magic can be used to cure as well as to hurt. Modern medicine uses the power of belief or suggestion all the time. Doctors have become increasingly aware of what is called the "placebo effect." A placebo is an inert medicine, say a pill made from sugar, but given an appropriately impressive shape and color.

Placebos are often used in study groups to test the effectiveness of new medicines. Half a group of patients will be given the new medicine while the other half will be given a placebo that looks exactly the same. Usually not even the doctors themselves are aware of which patients are getting the medicine and which the placebo. In a surprisingly large number of cases the placebo works as well as the medicine. The stronger the medicine is supposed to be, the better the placebo works. The placebo effect is entirely psychological; a placebo will not kill germs or mend a broken bone. If a sugar pill will make a sick person feel better today, just because he thinks that it should, then a magic charm would also make a sick person feel better, in a society where people believe in magic.

Magicians also dealt in herbs and other natural medicines. In many societies the magicians or tribal wizards were the only individuals who knew what herbs to pick and how to prepare them. Other members of the tribe were strictly forbidden to engage in such activity. By trial and error, down through the centuries the magicians found remedies that really worked. The magicians of some South American tribes would prepare a substance from the bark of certain trees and give it to people who suffered from malaria. This substance, called quinine, reduced the pain and fever of the disease better than any medicine known, and it was adopted by scientifically trained doctors.

Poison was another part of the tribal magician's stock in trade. An evil wizard's victim often died from poison rather than from any curse or spell.

A less well-known staple of the wizard's collection of potions and brews was hallucination-producing drugs. Central Asian shamans routinely burned hemp seeds, which produce narcotic fumes, at their ceremonies. Medieval magicians and witches prepared ointments containing extracts from plants of the nightshade family. When absorbed through the skin these substances can produce vivid and terrifying dreams.

The magician was often called upon to discover who was guilty of a crime. Here, too, magic frequently "worked." The suspects were told by the magician that they would have to undergo an ordeal which only the guilty party would fail. The ordeal might be difficult, for example, putting your hand in a fire, on the theory that only the guilty would be burned. Or it might be simple, swallowing a piece of bread, in the belief that the guilty would choke. No magic could prevent both innocent and guilty from being burned. But if the guilty party really believed in magic he might well break down and confess before the ordeal began. In the swallowing ordeal the guilty man might become so nervous that he could not swallow properly, while innocent persons swallowed quite easily.

Among the Bantus of Africa guilt detection requires the cooperation of an entire village. The suspects are lined up in front of the villagers who then begin to chant. As the witch doctor approaches a popular individual, the chanting dies down to a whisper, but when he gets near the person the community already believes to be guilty, the chant rises to an angry roar. The witch doctor can be assured of making a popular choice, and of increasing his own prestige. The villagers too are happy, for their suspicions seem to have been confirmed by a supernatural force. Similar methods were used in other parts of the world, and much of magic was concerned with encouraging a person to believe or do what he wanted to believe or do anyway.

Magic worked in more indirect ways, primarily because it gave people hope. In uncertain enterprises like war or primitive agriculture the magical rituals would stimulate the warriors or farmers to fight more fiercely or work harder. A warrior who believes that he

Chief of the Florida Indians consults a tribal wizard at the time of the arrival of the white men in America.

cannot lose, or a farmer who is convinced that his crops will not fail, is going to do his job better.

Naturally, very often magic didn't work. Then the magician always had a ready excuse for failure, and the magician's client was generally ready to accept the excuse. Occasionally wizards and magicians were executed or exiled when they failed, but this did not happen often.

Rumor undoubtedly played a major part in man's continuing belief in the power of magic. There were no consumer affairs committees to check out any particular wizard's claims. The wizard and his client were surely more willing to talk about successful spells than unsuccessful ones, and one apparent success would wipe out the memory of a hundred failures. As the tale of a particularly spectacular magical feat was repeated from village to village it grew more wonderful. The magicians themselves were often wanderers. If the inhabitants of one town or village became disillusioned, the wizard would move on to a new place, filled with eager and hopeful potential clients.

Who were the people who became magicians? In the beginning every man was probably his own magician, but later specialists in the magical arts developed. The first man in a tribe who used fire was doubtless considered a wizard by his contemporaries. Magical power might be acquired by birth, or by the possession of "secret knowledge." A combination of both produced the best magicians.

Any group that had trade secrets were liable to be considered magicians. In Africa the men who know how to smelt metals protect their secrets by elaborate and fearful rituals, most of which have nothing whatever to do with the practical business of smelting, but are aimed primarily at keeping outsiders from finding out what they are doing.

Anyone who was somehow "different" was a good candidate for magician. People who were born deformed might either be executed as demons, or raised to the status of magicians. Madmen who ran about shouting and muttering, or epileptics who were suddenly seized with convulsions, would seem like people who were in touch with the gods or spirits or possessed by supernatural entities. The magician was always an outsider. He dealt with things that it was dangerous for ordinary folk to meddle with. Magicians were often respected and feared, but rarely loved.

It was important for the magician to remain an outsider, as uncomfortable and even dangerous as that position might be. His magical secrets had to be protected. He lived in some remote and gloomy spot where most people did not like to go, and his dress was different from that of ordinary folk, often spectacularly so.

The magician was, and still is, by nature an actor, for much of magic depends on impressive theatrical effects. When magic ceased to be respectable the word magician came to be applied to a showman who fooled his audiences by illusions or tricks. Stage magic is an honorable and honest profession, though it is based on trickery. Everyone knows and accepts that the stage magician's effects are tricks, and we are entertained, even amazed, by his cleverness. The magician who used the same sort of tricks, but claimed that he possessed supernatural powers, would be a fraud. Some of those who passed themselves off as practitioners of "real magic" were just this sort of fraud, but it would be quite wrong to conclude that most magicians were tricksters. They often deliberately exaggerated their alleged powers and attempted to mystify people about what they were actually doing, but they believed in the power of magic.

3
THE ANCIENT MAGICIANS

FROM THE DAWN OF HISTORY TO THE CHRISTIAN ERA

MOST MODERN STUDENTS of magic look to ancient Egypt as the original home of all magic and mystery. Egyptian civilization is one of the oldest that we know. It began some 6,500 years ago, and continued without essential change for some 4,000 years. With Egypt the longest-lived civilization on record, it seemed reasonable to assume that the Egyptians possessed all sorts of magical secrets and traditions lost to others. But, unfortunately, we have only hints of the sort of magic used by the earliest of these people.

The first rulers of Egypt had their wives and many of their servants sacrificed and buried in their tombs when they died. The victims were supposed to continue to serve the king in the next world. But later in Egyptian history sacrificial victims were replaced by statues and tomb paintings of wives and servants. Magically, the images were supposed to fulfill the same function as the real people.

Inscriptions on tombs would exhort passersby to speak the name of the man buried within, so that he might magically gain strength in the next world.

In later ages the Egyptians composed stories about various great wizards who had lived in the early days. We have no definite knowledge of whether such individuals really existed. There is one exception, a man called Imhotep. He lived around the year 2700 B.C., and was an official in the court of the Pharaoh Zoser. When Zoser decided to build a new type of tomb for himself he appointed Imhotep to head the project. Under Imhotep's direction there emerged the Step Pyramid, the first of the Egyptian pyramids, and the largest freestanding stone monument built to that time.

Whether the people of the time regarded Imhotep as a wizard we don't know. Centuries after his death, he had not only picked up the reputation of wizard, he was often worshiped as a god. People commonly attribute all manner of deeds to great men of the past. Stories credited Imhotep with discovering writing, or the secrets of agriculture, or a lot of other things that were really discovered long before he lived.

It is not until we get to the Greeks that magicians begin to emerge as definite characters. The earliest of these that we know of were women.

GODDESSES AND WITCHES

From the twilight area between history and legend comes Circe, one of the first magicians in history whose name and deeds have been recorded. Homer wrote about her around the year 700 B.C.

On their long return home from the Trojan War, the hero Odysseus and his crew put in at the island of Aeaea. Venturing inland they found a stone house surrounded by mountain lions and wolves, all strangely docile and friendly. Inside the house lived a woman called Circe. Odysseus' men called her a goddess; later ages were to label her a witch. The early Greeks made no particular distinction between a good magician and an evil one. Circe was not regarded as evil, merely powerful.

Circe enticed the men into her house and fed them a meal of cheese, barley, and wine, with a little something special added. The men were immediately turned into swine and Circe shut them up in her pigsty. The beasts that surrounded her house had been previous dinner guests.

With aid from the gods Odysseus was able to force Circe to restore his men to human form. Still he spent a year with the enchantress before he was able to pull himself together and continue his journey home.

Although the Greeks themselves regarded Homer's poems as reasonably authentic history, later historians chose to believe them entirely fabulous. But it has turned out that much of what Homer wrote about did have a basis in historical fact. The fabulous island of Aeaea has been identified with a promontory in southern Italy called Circeii. It is possible that at some time in the dim past this spot was the home of a celebrated magician, and that her deeds were incorporated, in an exaggerated fashion, into the Homeric tale of Circe the goddess.

Circe's niece Medea "the cunning one" seems a more solid character, though the deeds attributed to her are no less miraculous. She was the daughter of Aeetes, king of the Colchians, and was universally acknowledged to be a witch (someone who used magic for evil purposes), though it seems in a few places she may have been worshiped as a goddess. Medea plays an important part in the legend of Jason and the Argonauts who went out in search of the golden fleece. Aeetes ordered Jason to perform an apparently impossible task, but Medea who was madly in love with the hero helped him accomplish the task by magic. Then she and Jason escaped Colchis, killing her young brother in the process. They had many adventures, including boiling an old man alive in a pot, before settling down in Corinth.

Though Medea made Jason swear never to love another woman, he went back on his word and decided to marry Creusa, a young princess. So Medea presented the bride elect with a deadly wedding gift, a garment which when put on burned her skin off and caused her to die in the most horrible agony. Then Medea killed the two children she had by Jason, and fled to Athens in her cart drawn by two dragons. In Athens she married Aegeus, but was exiled from the city after an attempt on the life of the hero Theseus. The legends generally have her finishing out her career in her homeland of Colchis.

Medea is not merely a witch or evil magician, she was the archetype of witch, yet despite her deeds the Greeks did not regard her as hateful. She was respected for her power, rather than despised for her evil. Though there were many magical characters in Greek mythology and legend, Medea is by far the most striking. Dozens and perhaps hundreds of local legends and stories crystallized around her. By the time her deeds were written down the historical Medea, if indeed there had been one, was completely obscured.

The people of the Greek district called Thessaly claimed that Medea lost her box of wonder-working plants over their land, and that was why Thessaly was especially famous for its production of magical herbs and magicians. There was a saying that, "the chant of the Thessalian witch penetrates the furthest seat of the gods and contains words so powerful that not the care of the skies, or of the revolving spheres, can avail as an excuse to the deities to decline its force."

Perhaps the most complete account of ancient witchcraft or magic on record was set down by the Roman writer Lucan who lived during the first century of the Christian era. Lucan described the visit of Sextus Pompey, son of Julius Caesar's adversary Pompey the Great, to a particularly horrid Thessalian witch named Erichtho. Sextus went to the witch to find out what the future held for him. Erichtho warned him that despite her powers she could not break the chain of fate, but that she could see the future through the use of necromancy—consulting the dead. Sextus was satisfied. "Though it may be well enough for the oracles and prophets who serve the Olympians to give riddling responses, a man who dares consult the dead deserves to be told the truth."

For Erichtho's magic to be successful she had to invoke the aura of death. She lived in an open grave surrounded by bones and pieces of corpses. To perform the ghastly ceremony she asked for a fresh dead body, "whose flexible organs shall yet be capable of speech, not with lineaments already hardened by the sun." Old corpses, she complained, "only squeak incoherently."

When a proper corpse was selected, "she passed a hook beneath the jaw of the selected one, and fastening it to a cord, dragged him along over rocks and stones until she reached a cave overhung by a projecting ridge. A gloomy fissure in the ground was there of a depth almost reaching to the Infernal Gods, where the yew tree spread thick its horizontal branches, at all times excluding the light of the sun."

Erichtho put on a colored robe, combed her hair over her face and adjusted her wreath of vipers. She then cut a hole in the dead man's chest and poured in a concoction of the most revolting imaginable ingredients, such as froth from the jaws of a mad dog, marrow of a stag fed on serpents, and hump of a corpse-fed hyena. Next she began to chant an incantation which "seemed to mingle the barking of dogs and howling of wolves, the screech of an owl, the roaring of wild beasts and hissing of snakes, the crash of waves on rocks, the murmur of forest trees and the bellow of thunder." All of the gods of darkness and the underworld, called euphemistically the Kindly Ones, were appealed to. Finally a ghost appeared, but refused at first to enter the corpse. So Erichtho threatened it with a long list of infernal powers, and also promised that when the ceremony was over the corpse would be burned so that it could no longer be used for magical purposes.

"The body raises itself, not by degrees, but at a single impulse, and stands erect. The eyelids unclose, the countenance is not that of a living subject, but of the dead. The paleness of the complexion, the rigidity of the lines, remain. And he looks about with an unmeaning stare . . ."

When the corpse answers the desired questions, "The sorceress constructs the funeral pyre; the dead man places himself thereon; Erichtho applies the torch; and the charm is for ever at an end."

Lucan was a poet writing long after the event he described was supposed to have taken place. The scene may be entirely fictional, and if not it is certainly exaggerated. Yet from what we know about the practice of magic, it is safe to infer that ceremonies of this sort must have been attempted. The belief that the dead could foresee the future is a very ancient one. In order to raise the dead one needed the symbols of death, hence Erichtho's use of open graves, gloomy places, and other things associated with death. Finally there is the fearful nature of the entire ceremony. Traditionally necromancy was the most dangerous and feared of all the magical arts. But even simple magic often had, and still has, an element of fear and evil clinging to it.

THE PYTHAGOREANS

Pythagoras, as every school child knows, was an ancient Greek mathematician. But he was also a mystic and a magician and founder of a strange but highly influential religiopolitical cult. He is one of the most important figures, both in the history of science and in the history of magic.

Unfortunately, there is very little that we genuinely know about Pythagoras. He was born on the Greek island of Samos sometime during the sixth century B.C. He is said to have traveled widely, particularly in Egypt, in search of universal truths. We next find Pythagoras as a middle-aged man back at Samos attempting to teach whatever it was he had learned to his fellow Greeks.

The only firm date we have for Pythagoras is the year 529 B.C. It was then that he left Samos to go to Crotona, a Greek colony in southern Italy, where he established his celebrated "brotherhood" (a misnomer, for it seems that women were admitted). The Pythagorean brotherhood was a secret society. The purpose of the brotherhood was to study the secrets of nature and magic as revealed by Pythagoras. They kept their secrets well, and only disconnected fragments of the original Pythagorean doctrines survive.

Those wishing to join the group had to go through a long period of initiation, presumably to purify their souls for the truths they were to receive. For years they were not even allowed to gaze directly upon Pythagoras, but had to hear his lectures through a curtain.

Pythagoras possessed the true sorcerer's love of appearing as an awesome and supernatural figure. He never came out in the daylight and appeared even to his most trusted disciples only at night. A later writer described him thus: "He appeared in a garment of the purest white, with a flowing beard and a garland upon his head. He is said to have been of the finest symmetrical form with majestic carriage and a grave and awful countenance. He suffered his followers to believe that he was one of the gods, the Hyperborean Apollo, and is said to have told Abaris [one of his disciples] that he had assumed human form that he might better invite men to an easiness of approach and to confidence in him." There were numerous accounts of the miracles he reportedly performed. He was said to be able to become invisible, walk upon water, and make objects miraculously appear and disappear.

Pythagoras claimed to have appeared in different ages in various human forms, and a belief in reincarnation (though not necessarily in human forms) may have been held by the cult as a whole. They preached kindness to animals, an important ethic for believers in reincarnation.

Numbers played an important part in the Pythagorean system. Numerology or number magic is popular even today, and it began with Pythagoras and his followers. The essence of numerology is that the number of a thing, like the name of the thing, has great magical significance. The most common application of numerology is trying to tell fortunes by finding the "root number" of a person's name. Each letter of the alphabet is assigned a number. (How these numbers were originally assigned we do not know, and there are many different systems in use today.) The numbers of all the letters in the person's name are then added up. If the total is a two-digit number like 14 then these two digits are added together, $1 + 4 = 5$, and 5 is the root number. One then finds the significance of five, and this is supposed to reveal something about the character and future of the person whose name is being investigated.

The Pythagoreans also used their numbers to make some very acute and very accurate scientific calculations and observations. Pythagoras may well have been the first man to postulate that the earth is a sphere.

The Pythagoreans practiced a number of primitive magical rituals. They were always supposed to put the sandal on the right foot first, but when washing their feet, they started with the left foot. Upon arising they were required to roll their bedclothes together and smooth out the impression of the place where they had been lying. When they cut their hair or nails, they were instructed to spit upon the cuttings. These practices indicate a belief in simple sympathetic magic. Among the Greeks, primitive magic was often mixed with sophisticated philosophy.

While Pythagoras carried on like a god among his disciples he had acquired a lot of enemies at Crotona. It seems that the Pythagorean brotherhood had become rich and powerful. In the complicated politics which were an inevitable part of all ancient Greek communities, Pythagoras had thrown the weight of his brotherhood behind the aristocratic party. When the aristocrats lost out, Pythagoras was in trouble. One story says he was exiled from Crotona, and died before he could return. Another says that he was burned to death trying to save his library when a mob attacked the headquarters of the brotherhood.

At about the time that Pythagoras was alive, another philosopher and miracle worker was active in Greece. His name was Epimenides. Though we have little authentic knowledge of Pythagoras we know even less about Epimenides. He seems to have held a philosophy similar to that of Pythagoras; at least ancient writers often linked the two. Epimenides was born on the island of Crete. The first extraordinary event in his life, according to the legends, was that he slept for fifty-seven years. As a youth he had been a shepherd, and while seeking a stray he wandered into a cave and fell asleep. He awoke thinking that he had slept only a few hours. When he returned to his father's house he discovered that his father had long since died, and the house had a new owner. Finally he managed to find his younger brother, by then an old man who barely recognized him. Epimenides had not aged during his long sleep, and the stories say that he lived to the age of one hundred and fifty-seven.

Epimenides made a variety of claims to supernatural powers. He said that he was fed by spiritual creatures, and did not need ordinary food. He said he could send his spirit out of his body whenever and wherever he wished, and he frequently claimed the ability to foresee the future.

The best documented feat attributed to Epimenides occurred about the year 600 B.C. There had been an unsuccessful revolt in Athens, and the rebels sought sanctuary in a temple. Their enemies lured them from the temple with a false promise and killed them. This was a flagrant violation of the ancient custom of sanctuary, and the people of Athens were shocked by the act. Even the gods seemed to strike out to punish this sacrilege. A plague broke out in the city, and ominous signs and portents were seen everywhere. The customary sacrifices and prayers accomplished nothing. Finally in desperation, the Athenian senate dispatched a special ship to Crete to fetch the great sage Epimenides.

Epimenides prescribed some fairly elaborate sacrifices, including, it was whispered, two humans. Whatever the remedy, it seemed to work, for the spread of the plague ended and the frightful apparitions were seen no more.

A more substantial figure was the philosopher and magician Apollonius, born in the Asia Minor city of Tyana, during the very early years of the Christian era. At the age of sixteen Apollonius entered a very rigorous cult of Pythagorean persuasion. He took vows of celi-

Apollonius of Tyana.

bacy and vegetarianism and wore nothing but a simple piece of linen cloth. For five years he swore he would not speak a word, and when he spoke again he had mastered all languages including those of the birds and animals. Barefoot and bearded, this ascetic scholar wandered widely in search of knowledge, performing miracles wherever he went.

He was well known as a healer and clairvoyant. When the unpopular Emperor Domitian was stabbed, Apollonius was heard to shout, "Strike, Strike! 'Tis done, the tyrant is no more!"—though he was many miles from the scene of the assassination.

At one city that was infested by plague, the people asked Apollonius to find the cause of the disease. The sage pointed to an aged beggar in the marketplace and said he was an evil spirit that should be stoned to death immediately. The people were reluctant to kill an apparently harmless old man, but Apollonius insisted, and soon the beggar was completely covered by a pile of stones that had been thrown at him. When the pile was removed, instead of finding the body of the beggar, the people found a huge black dog. Afterwards the pestilence ended.

A favorite disciple of the sage, a young man named Menippus, decided to marry a rich and beautiful woman whom he had met. Apollonius warned against the marriage, but would not exactly give his reasons, saying only that Menippus "nursed a serpent at his bosom." But the young man ignored the advice and went ahead with the marriage anyway. Apollonius was invited to the wedding feast and when he arrived he told Menippus that it was all an illusion, the guests, the plates of gold, even the wine he was drinking simply did not exist. To prove this he made them all disappear.

However, the bride herself did not disappear, and under prodding from Apollonius she admitted that she was a vampire and that the whole marriage had been a plot to eat Menippus's flesh and drink his blood.

The source of Apollonius's great powers and knowledge is uncertain. He seems to have claimed to have received both directly from the gods. Others asserted that he carried some magical rings given to him by a prince of India, and that the rings were the source of his power. It was believed that Apollonius lived to be nearly one hundred years old, and to have been one of the most widely respected and honored men of his time. Nothing is known of the manner or place of his death.

Years after Apollonius died, Julia, mother of the Emperor Severus, had a scribe gather up all that was known of Apollonius of Tyana and write his biography. It is the only surviving source of information about him, and is so full of obviously fictitious wonder stories that one is tempted to conclude that Apollonius himself was a fictional creation. But beneath all the romance there appears to be the outline of the life of a genuine historical figure, not so much a magician but a wandering pagan philosopher. He became popular with the pagans of Rome at the time that Christianity was gathering strength. Many miracles were ascribed to him to give him magical status equal to that of Jesus. (The Biblical accounts of the miracle of the loaves and the fishes, the raising of Lazarus, and walking upon water were magic to the pagans.) In fact, some anti-Christian writers drew direct parallels between the life of Jesus and that of Apollonius of Tyana, a comparison which enraged the early Christians. They countered by claiming that Apollonius had been placed upon earth by Satan in order to eclipse the miracles of Christ.

SIMON MAGUS AND THE GNOSTICS

In the New Testament Book of Acts 8:9–24 there is mention of a wizard named Simon.

"But there was a certain man, called Simon, which beforetime in the same city used sorcery, and bewitched the people of Samaria, giving out that he himself was some great one:

"To whom they all gave heed, from the least to the greatest, saying, This man is the great power of God.

"And to him they had regard, because that of long time he had bewitched them with sorceries."

The apostles Peter and John came to Samaria, and Simon was very impressed with the healing miracles that they performed.

"And when Simon saw that through laying on of the apostles' hands the Holy Ghost was given, he offered them money,

"Saying, Give me also this power, that on whomsoever I lay hands, he may receive the Holy Ghost.

"But Peter said unto him, Thy money perish with thee, because thou has thought that the gift of God may be purchased with money.

"Thou hast neither part nor lot in this matter: for thy heart is not right in the sight of God."

That is just about all the Bible has to say about Simon the wizard. However, early Christian commentators were quick to embellish the story of his life. He was said to be able to make himself invisible, to assume the appearance of another person or of an animal, to walk through fire, to make statues move, call up demons, fly through the air, walk through solid rock, and so on through an exhaustive list of miraculous performances.

Why, one might wonder, would such a wizard desire the power of the apostles? Said the commentators, Simon complained that his sorceries took too much time and trouble because he had to go through tedious rites and incantations. He wanted to perform miracles with just a few words, or with the "laying on of hands" as the apostles could.

Simon was said to have learned his magic from a false messiah named Dositheus, who had lived at the time of Christ. Later Simon himself was to attempt a messianic role.

St. Clement, one of the early popes, described how Simon went to Rome where he was immediately beheaded on the orders of the Emperor Nero. Then Nero realized that he had made a mistake and had the wizard's head placed back on his shoulders. Thus restored to life Simon became Nero's court sorcerer. So great did Simon's influence become that Peter feared he would disrupt the spread of Christianity into Rome. Peter himself went to the city to combat the wizard. Nero regarded Peter as a rival wizard, and brought the two together for a magical contest. Simon performed all manner of miracles and topped off his performance by sailing gracefully through a window of the palace and out over the streets of Rome. Peter retaliated by a loud prayer which caught Simon in midflight and sent him crashing to earth. Nero had Peter imprisoned, but Simon died as a result of the fall.

The story is obviously fabulous, but the early Church Fathers delighted in relating how the apostles and saints were able to outperform the magicians and wizards. Who the biblical Simon was we cannot be sure, but the early Christians were quick to identify him with one of their most formidable opponents, a prophet who was known as Simon Magus (Simon the Wise or Simon the Magician).

Simon Magus was one of the earliest known leaders of a religious system called Gnosticism. The name comes from the Greek word *gnosis* or knowledge. The origins of Gnosticism are obscure, but it probably started during the very early years of Christianity. Gnosticism grew into a complicated set of beliefs, drawing not only upon Christian and Jewish thought but on Oriental religion and pagan philosophy as well. It is really quite impossible to say with any precision what the Gnostics believed, for little Gnostic literature survived, and practically everything we know about them comes from the writings of their bitter enemies, the orthodox Christians.

There are, however, two prominent features of Gnostic belief that contributed to Simon's magical reputation. First was the Gnostic idea that the god worshiped by the Christians was not the true god, but that there was an Unknown God who had revealed his presence secretly to the Gnostics through the disciples of Jesus. The Christians naturally assumed that this Unknown God was the Devil and, since they also believed that magical power could come from the Devil, Simon was accused of being a magician and Devil worshiper.

Second, there was the concept of the *gnosis*, the secret knowledge itself. Any secret knowledge was simply assumed to be magical.

Left: Medieval drawing showing either the reign of Antichrist or the conflict between Simon Magus and St. Peter.

Were the Simon of the Bible and Simon the Gnostic one and the same? Probably not. The biblical Simon seems to have been some obscure magician of Samaria, whom the apostles had encountered in their travels. Later ages identified him with the more famous Simon, prophet of the Gnostics and powerful opponent of Christianity.

Did Simon the Gnostic himself practice magic? Most probably he did. Numerology, invoking the spirits to provide supernatural aid, making magical charms, and similar practices were common among the peoples of the Middle East during the first years of the Christian era. Both Christians and Jews of the time believed in the power of magic. They simply thought that to attempt to practice magic without divine aid was evil. If God wasn't helping the magician, then the magician must be getting his power from the Devil. Simon and his followers were heavily influenced by Oriental religions and cults, where the practice of magic was not regarded as evil.

As a separate religious movement Gnosticism died out centuries ago. However, some basic Gnostic ideas kept turning up in heretical Christian sects until nearly modern times.

Modern occultists claim that some of the magical knowledge possessed by the Gnostics has been passed on secretly from century to century. For example, they claim that the popular fortune-telling tarot cards are filled with Gnostic symbols. One of the most enigmatic cards in the tarot deck is called the Juggler. This, say the occultists, stands for the Unknown God of Gnosticism. Both the card of the Emperor, creator of things in this world, and the Pope, creator of things spiritual, at least in the sense of conventional Christianity, are supposed to be evil because they oppose the Unknown God.

From Egypt have come a huge number of precious and semiprecious stones engraved with strange figures and Greek letters. These are called Gnostic amulets and talismans and were believed to be es-

Engraved jewels and cameos attributed to the Gnostics. The significance of the various designs is unknown.

pecially powerful charms. But we don't really know what the figures mean.

In fact, we know virtually nothing of the real magical beliefs and practices of the Gnostics. But the belief in unknown forces and secret knowledge links them firmly to the tradition of magic.

4
MEDIEVAL MAGIC

FROM THE RISE OF CHRISTIANITY TO THE SEVENTEENTH CENTURY

THE CHRISTIAN CHURCH TRIUMPHED over the followers of Simon Magus. The deeds of Apollonius of Tyana were put into the shadows. The pagan barbarians who could not be conquered were slowly converted. In Western Europe at least, the triumph of Christianity seemed complete. The popular belief grew that Europe during the Middle Ages lived in an age of faith, peasants, and nobles piously committed to a church that was both ruler and civilizer. The true picture, however, was far more complicated.

Many of those who converted to Christianity did so only because they were forced, or because they found it convenient. Basically they remained pagans, and they accepted the Christian God as just one more in a vast pantheon of gods to be worshiped and appeased. At first the Church had neither the power nor the desire to make an issue of the many survivals of pagan beliefs among those who professed to be Christian. Such beliefs were tolerated, and if possible incorporated into Christianity itself. The pagan celebration of spring became part of the Christian celebration of Easter; the ancient rituals surrounding the winter solstice were incorporated into the celebration of Christmas. The pagan hero Perseus who had slain a sea monster was to become St. George, the slayer of the dragon.

Among the common folk in Christian lands magic was practiced just as it always had been. Magic was personal and immediate. The magician promised his clients cures for their diseases, recovery of their lost property, love from those whom they desired, and many other immediate rewards. The Church referred all man's needs and desires to God's inscrutable mercy.

The line between religion and magic, however, was not as sharp in practice as in theory. Medieval Catholicism had many magical facets. The miracles attributed to the saints did not sound any different than the feats of magic attributed to great pagan magicians and gods. There was some dispute among Christians as to whether the time of miracles was past. Most people agreed that it wasn't and miracles could still happen. Learned theologians pointed out that a prayer was not the same as a spell, that the Mass was not a magical rite, and holy relics were not amulets or talismans, but such theological distinctions were lost on the common folk. To them a priest, praying in Latin (a language they did not understand) for the recovery of a sick man, was not very different from the village magician who uttered equally incomprehensible spells. The magicians themselves often invoked the aid of the "Father, Son, and Holy Ghost" in their spells, and gave their clients magical pieces of paper upon which were written fragments of Latin prayers. In medieval England magicians were often called "blessers." The cross was regarded as a powerful talisman, used for warding off all manner of evil spirits. Priests, who themselves were often no better educated than the people they served, believed as they did, and willingly acted as "holy magicians." They regarded the wizards not as representatives of old and outworn beliefs, but as powerful rivals. People were admonished not to seek the services of

A saint combats the diabolical enchantments of a magician.

magicians, but for centuries the magician and his clients had little trouble with the church so long as they remained modest and quiet.

Official Church condemnation of magic grew slowly. The Emperor Constantine who legitimized Christianity in the year A.D. 313 specifically forbade certain types of magic, and ordered the severest penalties for those "charming the minds of modest persons to the practice of debauchery." But there was no prohibition against magic in general. Civil authorities were always free to take action against "black magicians," those whose spells and charms were aimed at harming their neighbors. But those magicians who concentrated on curing disease, finding lost objects, or protecting clients from the spells of evil magicians, were either ignored or respected.

The Crusades against the Moslems in the Holy Land were launched early in the eleventh century. They failed, but the crusading spirit did not die out. The Church sponsored a series of crusades against heretical sects in Christian lands. Heresy had been punishable by death since the fifth century, but the penalty had rarely been enforced. In 1184 Pope Lucius III called together his bishops and ordered a systematic inquiry or *inquisito* into any deviation from the official teachings of the Church. Thus began that notorious body that came to be known as the Inquisition, which, in several centuries of unbelievably bloody warfare and appalling persecutions, succeeded in exterminating all of the major heretical sects of Western Europe.

The step from persecution for heresy to persecution for magic is a natural one. The orthodox Christian believed in the power of magic. There were only two possible sources of such power, God and the Devil. God could be reached only through His Church; thus all of those who possessed magical power and were outside of the Church must have obtained it from the Devil. The heretical sects had always been accused of practicing magic, but it was their heresy, not their magic, for which they were condemned. Then in 1451 the Inquisition was allowed to extend its authority to deal with all sorts of magic, even if it did not "manifestly savor of heresy."

Soon the Church came to regard all magic as a crime, as "witchcraft." Inquisitors recalled the biblical injunction, "Thou shalt not suffer a witch to live." It made no difference whether the accused witch was supposed to have tried to harm his or her neighbors by black witchcraft, or help them by white witchcraft. It didn't even matter whether the magic worked. The crime was not the magic it-

A sorcerer condemned to death by the Inquisition. A condemned man was forced to wear a robe illustrating his crime.

self, but the assumption that the witch had made a pact with the Devil. Indeed, many theologians regarded the white witch as the more dangerous. The evil or black witch was obvious and could harm only a person's body. But the white witch with her (most accused witches were women) helpful charms and spells might seduce a man away from God and thus endanger his immortal soul. For nearly three centuries Europe was swept by a periodic madness that might be called the "witch mania." Countless thousands of perfectly harmless village cunning men and women, as magicians were often called, as well as an unknown number of people who had nothing whatever to do with magic, were tortured and executed for the "crime" of witchcraft. Both Catholics and Protestants were enthusiastic participants in the horrible sport of witch-hunting.

Yet this ferocious activity did not end the practice of magic. The persecution of witches was neither well-organized nor consistent. Much depended upon local conditions, and the disposition of a particular noble or bishop. Except where the hysteria was unusually severe, witches who had good reputations in their communities could operate in relative safety. Indeed, the witchcraft hysteria often increased their business, for people became so frightened of bad witches that they ran to the good witches for protection.

The magic employed by village cunning men and women was drawn from a variety of sources, some of them quite ancient. Take, for example, the word "abracadabra." This word has been used so often that the dictionary defines it as a term for magical mumbo jumbo. But for centuries it was thought to be a powerful magical charm.

The first known mention of the word comes from Quintus Serenus Sammonicus, a doctor who was with the Roman Emperor Severus on his expedition to Britain in A.D. 208. Quintus said that the word, written on a piece of paper in the form of a triangle, should be hung around the neck of a person suffering from fever. The usual way of writing the word was:

A B R A C A D A B R A
A B R A C A D A B R
A B R A C A D A B
A B R A C A D A
A B R A C A D
A B R A C A
A B R A C
A B R A
A B R
A B
A

In nine days the patient's fever was supposed to shrink away to nothing, just as the word did. Then the paper was to be thrown backwards over the patient's shoulder into a stream running eastward.

This particular charm was still widely used in England fifteen centuries after it was first mentioned by the Roman doctor.

One of the most popular magical plants of the Middle Ages was the mandrake. Belief in the magical powers of the mandrake is extremely ancient. It was used by the ancient Greeks, and quite possibly by the Persians before them.

One reason the mandrake was thought to be magical is that its root often resembles a human figure. Another is that mandrake root contains a narcotic juice which can cause delirium and even death.

The mandrake was thought to be so powerful that it was dangerous for a human being to pull it out of the earth. In the middle of the night the magician would carefully loosen the mandrake root. Then he would tie a rope to the plant, and tie the other end of the rope around the neck of a black dog. The magician would then get out of the way and toss pieces of meat just out of the dog's reach. The straining dog would pull the root from the ground. The magician had carefully stuffed his ears with wax, because it was said that when a mandrake is torn from the ground it utters a terrible screech, which no man can hear and live. The dog is killed by the mandrake's cry and buried in its place.

A properly prepared mandrake root could then be used in a love potion, as a cure for gout, for inducing pregnancies in barren women, or for a host of other magical purposes.

Even while priests and magistrates were busily hunting down old women who used herbs and charms, a new magical development began to take place among the educated. This was the development of scholarly magic, or high magic as opposed to low magic or the magic of the common people. The village cunning men or women did not think much about the magic they practiced. Generally they repeated incantations or rituals that had been handed down by word of mouth for generations. They did not speculate much about the origins of magic.

The scholars, however, partly through reading ancient authors, and partly through their own speculations, built up a picture of a world in which there was little difference between matter and spirit. Says Keith Thomas, an historian of magic, "The Earth itself was deemed to be alive. The universe was peopled by a hierarchy of spirits, and thought to manifest all kinds of occult influences and sympathies. The cosmos was an organic unity in which every part bore a sympathetic relationship to the rest. Even colours and numbers were endowed with magical properties. The investigation of such phenomena was the primary task of the natural philosopher, and their employment for his own purposes was the distinguishing mark of the magician. Three main types of magical activity thus lay open: natural magic, concerned to exploit the occult properties of the elemental world; celestial magic, involving the influence of the stars; and ceremonial magic, an appeal for their aid to spiritual beings."

Most of the scholarly magicians were also Christians, and they fitted their magic to their Christian beliefs. The more Christian one sounded, the less trouble one was likely to get into. In one view, magic had been part of man's knowledge of nature that had been lost by Adam after the Fall. Portions of this knowledge had been passed on by certain "adepts," among them biblical figures like Moses, Solomon, and Enoch, as well as classical philosophers like Plato.

So popular was the study of magic, that the terms "scholar" and "magician" became virtually synonymous. In Shakespeare's play *Hamlet* one of the soldiers who spies a ghost turns to his companion and says, "Thou art a scholar; speak to it, Horatio." The line is puzzling to modern audiences, but it was perfectly clear to sixteenth-century Englishmen. They assumed that scholars knew all about dealing with ghosts and spirits.

The legend of the magician Faust clearly shows how people of the late Middle Ages and Renaissance regarded both magicians and scholars. Faust was said to be an extremely learned man who after years of study had discovered the method for conjuring up the Devil. He then exchanged his soul for worldly power and wealth.

There was a real Johann Faust by the way, but he seems to have been a rather commonplace magical pretender who lived in Germany during the early sixteenth century. The Faustian legend grew up in the years following the death of the historical Faust out of popular beliefs about magic and scholars.

The names and deeds of the countless village magicians are largely lost. We have only hints of who they were and what they did, like this English document written in 1638:

> "You have heard of Mother Nottingham, who for her time was prettily well skilled in casting of waters [a method of fortune-telling], and after her, Mother Bombay; and then there is one Hatfield in Pepper Alley, he doeth pretty well for a thing that's lost. There's another in Coleharbour that's skilled in the planets [astrology]. Mother Sturton in Golden Lane is for fore-speaking [prophecy]; Mother Phillips, of the Bankside for the weakness of the back; and then there's a very reverend matron on Clerkenwell Green good at many things."

Often the names of these simple practitioners of magic appear in the records only when they were accused of witchcraft or some other crime. The really successful wizards were never caught and are completely unknown. The scholarly magicians, on the other hand, are a much more vivid lot, and we will look at some of the most famous among them.

Faust summons up the Devil.

ROGER BACON

Roger Bacon was a scholar, one of the most formidable of his time. But his time was the thirteenth century, and any scholar who ventured to push his inquiries beyond the narrow limits laid down by the medieval Church was likely to be considered a sorcerer. So it was that Bacon developed the reputation of being a wonder worker who possessed the knowledge and power to control the elements, see the future, and put the Devil himself to flight.

Bacon was born in Somerset, England, around the year 1214. His genius was recognized when he was a boy and he was persuaded to join the Franciscan Order in about 1247. At that time the only career for a scholar lay within the Church. Bacon studied and lectured in Paris, until the year 1250 when he returned to England. What happened to him in England is not clear, but for some years after his return he took no part in the outward affairs of Oxford University where he resided. Perhaps the authorities were suspicious of his unorthodox views, or perhaps he was in poor health.

For fourteen years, from 1277 until 1291, Bacon was back in Paris and very probably in a Parisian jail because of his independent opinions, criticism of his superiors, and general quarrelsomeness. He was released just a year before his death, and returned to Oxford where he spent his final days.

During his lifetime Roger Bacon wrote prolifically on theology, mathematics, alchemy (medieval chemistry), and natural philosophy. He has been hailed as a prophet of experimental science as opposed to revelation, but the praise is misplaced, and based on a misunderstanding of his beliefs. Roger Bacon was a devout Christian for all his apparent unorthodoxy. He even went out of his way to ridicule some of the magical pretensions of his day. Yet in the thirteenth century the line between such studies as natural philosophy, theology, and magic was by no means clear. In later ages, both scientists and magicians were to claim Bacon as one of their own, a unique double distinction. The magicians hailed Bacon as a member of that long line of semidivine magical "adepts."

By the sixteenth century, when magic was studied seriously, Bacon was probably better known than he had been in his own time. There was a popular book entitled *The History of Friar Bacon.* A play based upon the incidents in the book was regularly performed in Elizabethan times.

In the book and play Bacon is the perfect Christian magician, modest, yet supremely powerful. When he is called before the king he disclaims any real knowledge or power. He then proceeds to give the royal party a dazzling display of conjuring by calling up dancers, a full banquet, rare perfumes, and many other things by a mere wave of his hand.

Friar Bacon was also credited with saving a man who had sold his soul to the Devil. The man had been deeply in debt, and agreed to deliver up his soul if the Devil would give him enough money to satisfy all his creditors. The Devil said he would claim the man's soul when all his debts were paid. The debtor did the best he could to pay up slowly, but finally he could stall no longer. In desperation he consulted Friar Bacon who instructed him to meet the Devil the next morning and contest the claim to his soul. He was then to offer to refer the dispute to the first person who passed by. The man did as Bacon suggested, and the Devil agreed to allow the first person who passed to judge their case. At this point Bacon, who had been hiding in the woods, popped out.

The Devil explained his case and demanded justice. Bacon then asked the terrified gentleman if he had ever paid the Devil any of his money back. "Never had he anything of me as yet," answered the gentleman.

"Then never let him have anything of thee, and thou are free. Deceiver of mankind," said Bacon turning to the Devil, "it was thy bargain never to meddle with him so long as he was indebted to any; now how canst thou demand of him anything when he is indebted for all that he hath to thee? When he payeth thee thy money, then take

The Order of the Illuminiti, supposedly one of the groups of magical adepts. This group included Apollonius of Tyana, Mohammed, Roger Bacon, Edward Kelly, John Dee, and Paracelsus.

him as thy due; till then thou has nothing to do with him, and so I charge thee to be gone." The astonished and angry Devil vanished.

As is usual in such stories of deals with the Devil the fiend is portrayed as being extraordinarily stupid. This tale of Friar Bacon and the Devil seems to be an adaptation of a much older medieval story told about some other magical figure, but it does indicate the popular notion about Bacon's character and powers.

Though there was great admiration for Bacon's supposed magical talents, it was not considered correct or godly for mere magic to be rewarded. So the *History* has Bacon repenting. He had a magic glass by which he could see the future. One day two young noblemen who had been friends killed one another over what they saw in the glass. Bacon was so shocked that he broke the magic mirror.

He then heard that two other wonder-working friars had killed one another trying to prove which was the greater magician. Bacon became depressed, burned all his books on magic and distributed the money he had accumulated to the poor. Say the legends, Roger Bacon died as a hermit.

CORNELIUS AGRIPPA

The many enemies of Cornelius Agrippa claimed that he was always attended by a demon in the shape of a large black dog. They said that at the end of his life Agrippa made the inevitable deathbed confession and repented of all his ungodly acts of magic. He seized the dog and removed its collar which was covered with occult symbols. "Begone, wretched animal," Agrippa cried, "which has been the cause of my entire destruction." The dog plunged into the river and was seen no more.

"Nonsense," retorted Agrippa's disciple Johann Weyer. Certainly Agrippa had a pet dog, one that he treated with extraordinary kindness, even allowing it to eat at his table. But all this talk of demons was ignorant and superstitious slander. Weyer was, of course, correct, but it is hardly surprising that a lot of people chose to regard

Agrippa as an intimate of demons. Indeed, he often seemed to delight in encouraging his reputation as a demoniac sorcerer. Agrippa was no intimate of demons, but he was a magician.

Henry Cornelius Agrippa von Nettesheim was born in Cologne, Germany, in 1486. While still young, he built up a considerable reputation as both a scholar and soldier. As a scholar he was, naturally, well versed in astrology, alchemy, and natural philosophy, all of which were on the fringes of magic.

Like most other magical types, Agrippa thought very well of himself, and very poorly of anyone who had the temerity to disagree with him. The result was that he was almost constantly in trouble of one sort or the other. He was forced to leave his professorship at the University of Dole in France after a religious argument with a monk who accused him of heresy. In Italy his disputes with the clergy became so heated that he decided it best to get out of the country entirely.

At the city of Metz, where Agrippa was appointed advocate general, he courageously defended a young peasant girl who had been accused of witchcraft, and ultimately he won the case. But the witch-hunters would not forgive him and he was driven from that city as well.

Agrippa became court physician and astrologer to Louisa of Savoy, mother of the King of France, but she didn't like the horoscopes he was giving her, and so he was again out of a job. The most secure time of his career came when Margaret of Austria was his patron. The two got on well, and during that tranquil period Agrippa wrote most of his important works including the three volume *De occulta philosophia* (Occult Philosophy), the most complete collection of magical and occult knowledge ever composed.

After Margaret's death he was again forced to wander, and was briefly imprisoned either for debt or sorcery. Agrippa died at Grenoble, France, in 1534 at the age of forty-eight. His enemies said he died in wretched poverty, while his friends contend that he died amid luxury in the house of a wealthy patron.

After his death the stories of the miracles or sorceries he had per-

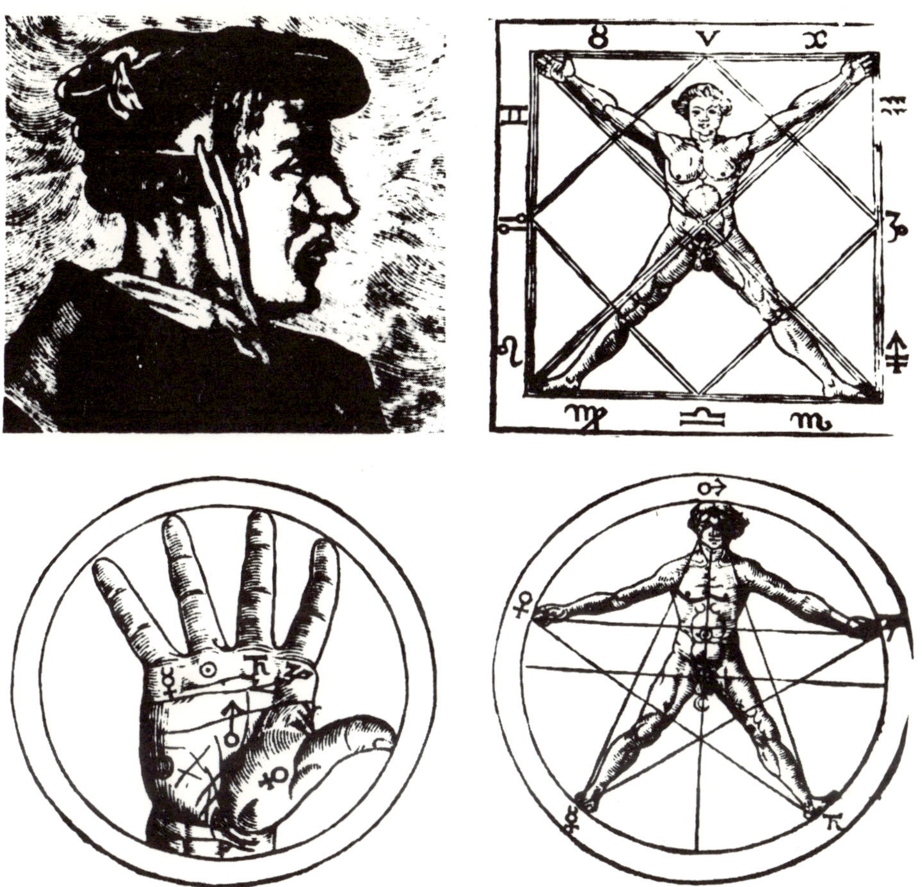

Cornelius Agrippa, and some of the drawings from his book on occult philosophy.

formed multiplied. Though the magician was continually dogged by debt, many believed that he had discovered the alchemical secret of transmuting base metals into gold. It was also said that when Agrippa paid a bill the money he used turned into worthless junk within an hour after he departed.

His feats of conjuring up spirits were endlessly repeated. He was said to have brought back the spirit of the Roman orator Cicero to entertain a group of distinguished men.

"After marshaling the concourse of spectators, Tully [Cicero] appeared at the command of Agrippa, and from the rostrum pronounced the oration, precisely in the words in which it has been handed down to us, with such astonishing animation, so fervent an exaltation of spirit, and such soul-stirring gestures, that all the persons present were ready, like the Romans of old, to pronounce his client innocent of every charge that had been brought against him."

Then there was the grimly amusing story of the student who, coming upon an open book on Agrippa's desk, accidentally read out a spell for conjuring up a demon. The demon, infuriated that he had been summoned for no reason, killed the student. When Agrippa returned home he found his house full of demons and the dead student on the floor. Agrippa feared that people would accuse him of murdering the student, so he commanded the chief demon to reanimate the boy's body and walk about with it in the marketplace while he ostentatiously stayed at home. Agrippa hoped that when the body suddenly fell lifeless to the street no one could accuse him of murder. However, so the story goes, the people suspected Agrippa anyway and he was driven from the town.

Such fables, many of which were centuries old, inevitably attach themselves to a man like Agrippa. But Agrippa did make some genuine contributions to the history of magic. When his greatest work, *De occulta philosophia*, finally was published over the objections of the Inquisition, it was enormously influential with other magic scholars.

Agrippa was no simple village cunning man or credulous believer in all magic. To a friend he wrote, "What surprising accounts we meet with, and how great writings there are made of the invincible power of the Magic Art; of the prodigious images of astrologers; of the amazing transmutations of the alchemists . . . all of which are found to be vain, fictitious and false, as often as they are practiced literally . . . yet such things are delivered and writ by great and grave philosophers, whose traditions who dares to say are false? No, it would be impious to think them lies. There is another meaning than what is written in bare words."

The three volumes of *De occulta philosophia* are filled with weighty speculations about harmonies, correspondences, and the other elements of magical philosophy. To this day Agrippa's books are basic texts for serious students of magic or the occult, but they do not provide a practical guide for the magician who is interested in conjuring up a spirit, making a love potion, or performing any other practical service for his clients. Far more popular than this three-volume work was a fourth volume, a *grimorie*, or magical handbook, attributed to Agrippa. This was filled with spells and incantations and all sorts of other useful magical information. But Agrippa never wrote such a book, and would have scorned the brand of simpleminded magic that it contained. The book was published long after his death and was a collection of magical lore that had been attributed to the famed scholar by an enterprising publisher. Agrippa's friends denounced the book as a hoax, but it did no good. On the strength of Agrippa's name alone the "fourth book" became the best-selling *grimorie* of the late sixteenth and seventeenth centuries. It is a sad fate for the great scholar of high magic to be best known as the author of a handbook of low magic.

JOHN DEE

When he had become quite old, John Dee confessed to the Holy Roman Emperor Rudolph II that for forty years he had sought knowledge through study, but had discovered that there was no book, and no living man who could tell him what he wanted to know. He decided, therefore, that the only way he could get the knowledge that he desired was by direct revelation from the spirits, whom he was always careful to call holy angels.

John Dee was the most famous magic scholar of the sixteenth century, and there is no doubt that he studied magic. In Bacon's time, and even as late as Agrippa, it was often impossible to separate magic from other branches of knowledge. By Dee's time the separation was clear.

Dee was born in England in 1527. Like Bacon and Agrippa he was a genius, and applied himself to his books for up to eighteen hours a day. In common with other scholars he studied such things as astrology and alchemy, still perfectly respectable subjects in the sixteenth century. But he also delved deeply into more esoteric branches of magic, and while still a student he had picked up something of a reputation as a wizard. He produced a play at Oxford which had some spectacular stage effects. In one scene a man flew off into the sky on the back of a giant beetle. Many people simply assumed he had used magic.

Dee became involved in the turbulent religious and political struggles of Tudor England. He was a Protestant, though not a very devout one, and was quite willing to pose as a Catholic when necessary. He was given a generous pension by Henry VIII's Protestant son Edward VI. But Edward died young and his successor, the very Catholic Mary, had the scholar arrested for treason. It seems that Dee had already been in contact with the household of Mary's sister and rival, Elizabeth. Perhaps he had been casting horoscopes for the princess indicating that she would one day attain the throne. Such an act could easily be regarded as treasonous, but nothing was ever proved against him. However, Dee's religious views were deemed sufficiently heretical for him to be imprisoned for a few years anyway.

Since Dee had been an early supporter of Elizabeth, when she came to the throne in 1558 he became virtually the royal wizard-in-chief. He calculated the astrologically proper moment for the queen's coronation. When a waxen image stuck full of pins was found near the queen's residence, John Dee was called in to use counter magic.

The scholar was accomplished in areas other than magic. He was very interested in navigation and the newly discovered continent of

Edward Kelly and an associate summon up the spirit of a dead person.

America. By his historical researches Dee tried to prove that America had once been part of the realm of King Arthur, thus strengthening the English claim to the New World. He worked to reform the archaic English calendar, and to promote a national library. Still, magic remained his chief passion.

Ultimately Dee confronted the crisis faced by most scholars of magic. No matter how much he studied he was never able to make his magic work. This did not shake his faith in magic, it merely made him change his methods. He had in his possession a crystal ball, and spent hours staring into it in the hope of having some sort of vision. On May 25, 1581, he recorded in his diary that he first perceived spirits in the crystal. In November of the following year he was sitting in his study when he saw a great burst of light in the west window. In the midst of the light stood the angel Uriel. Dee was unable to speak. The angel presented him with a new crystal and told him that whenever he wanted to converse with the angels he need only look into the crystal.

But there was a hitch. In order to see angels in the crystal Dee had to work himself into a state of mystic exaltation. When the state passed he was unable to remember anything he had seen or heard, a most unsatisfactory state of affairs.

Dee tried to employ scryers or professional crystal gazers, but they could see nothing in his marvelous crystal. Then along came Edward Kelly, who in everybody's opinion was a thoroughgoing villain. Kelly had already lost his ears after being convicted of forgery, and he was widely suspected of practicing necromancy and other black arts. Yet when he came to Dee he posed as a humble student, eager to sit at the feet of the great man. Soon, however, Kelly discovered he had a real knack for scrying. When Kelly was around spirits and angels appeared regularly in Dee's crystal and delivered ringing pronouncements and predictions. Dee himself saw nothing; he merely sat in a corner and wrote down what Kelly described to him.

Both Dee and Kelly were engaged in alchemy, an attractive but extremely expensive pursuit. In 1583 a Polish count visited Dee's home in the hope of discovering the alchemical secret of turning base metals into gold. The angels, speaking as usual through Kelly, promised that not only would the count be able to make gold, but that he would find the elixir of life, which would allow him to live forever, and that he would become king of Poland and accomplish many other great things.

The nobleman invited Dee and Kelly to continue their experiments on his estates in Poland, and the pair agreed. They may well have been anxious to get out of England at that moment, since there was a witchcraft panic building up, and they didn't want to be caught in it.

Though Queen Elizabeth liked John Dee, she could not be counted upon to protect him. The Queen maintained her power by appeasing the different powerful institutions in her realm. At that time the clergy was taking a hard line against magic, and the Queen could not afford to antagonize them. She would have watched Dee go to the stake, with regret no doubt, but without lifting a finger to save him. Dee was wise enough to know this, and to calculate that it would be safer to be on the Continent and give the English witchcraft panic time to blow over.

The two English wizards proved to be very expensive guests. They lived in almost royal splendor on the count's money. He also spent huge sums to finance their alchemical experiments. But the gold that Dee and Kelly had promised as the end result of these experiments never appeared. Dee and Kelly offered one excuse after the other to explain their failure. Finally in July of 1584 the Polish count sent them off with a letter of introduction to Emperor Rudolf II at Prague. Rudolf was known for his devotion to the practice of alchemy, but he was not much impressed by Dee and Kelly. The Catholic church, which had never been friendly to magicians, began to look with increasing suspicion at the two Englishmen, and the pair felt an urgent need to find a new and powerful protector. They visited the court of King Stephan of Poland, but he thought they were frauds.

Dee and Kelly began to look to England again. They sent Queen Elizabeth a brass warming pan with a gold disk in it. Dee said that

Kelly had turned the brass cutout into gold. The Queen was pleased, but she still did not invite them back to England. Dee also hinted that before he left England he had discovered a substance that allowed him to turn base metals into gold at Glastonbury Abbey, an ancient English shrine.

Finally Dee and Kelly found a new patron, a wealthy Bohemian nobleman named Count Rosenberg. But they did not stay in Bohemia long, for the partnership between the old scholar and his unscrupulous assistant had always been stormy, and it finally broke up.

Kelly took off to try his luck with the Emperor Rudolf again, but the emperor was no more impressed than he had been the first time. Kelly was jailed briefly for sorcery, released, and then after several years as an itinerant alchemist and fortune-teller he was jailed again. This time the charge was heresy, and Edward Kelly seemed doomed to spend the rest of his life in jail. In February, 1595, Kelly tried to escape from the tower in which he had been imprisoned, by lowering himself down on a rope. The rope broke and Kelly died from the injuries sustained in the fall.

Dee returned to England at the head of a great retinue of servants. Where he got the money for such a splendid return no one seems to know, and he spent at such a rate that his funds were soon gone. During his absence his reputation in England had declined as part of a general reaction against magic. A mob had ransacked his home and burnt some of his precious books while he had been away. Queen Elizabeth turned a deaf ear to his pleas for money, and her successor James was even less interested in helping the old scholar. Now a pathetic figure, John Dee was forced to support himself as a common fortune-teller. He even sold some of his remaining books to buy food. He died in 1608 at the age of eighty-one.

Modern scholars of magic assert that early in his career Dee had possessed some genuine magical knowledge, but that he wanted to know too much. Once under Kelly's influence he became more charlatan than scholar, and lost whatever powers he may once have possessed.

5
THE ALCHEMISTS

FROM THE BEGINNING OF THE CHRISTIAN ERA TO THE EIGHTEENTH CENTURY

THE WORD ALCHEMIST conjures up the picture of an ancient and bearded man bent over his crucibles and retorts in his endless quest to turn lead into gold. The picture, though accurate, is incomplete.

The transmutation of base metals into gold was only one small part of the alchemical quest, although it was always a popular and spectacular part. The true goal of the alchemist was the philosopher's stone.

To the alchemist and most of his contemporaries, the universe was unified and harmonious and pervaded by a "universal spirit." This belief could be summed up in the statement "One is All, and All is One." The alchemical problem was to somehow concentrate and purify matter, to a substance that contained the "universal spirit" in its pristine form. This was the philosopher's stone.

Though there were many stories of alchemists who had distilled the philosopher's stone as the result of their experiments, there is no reliable evidence that the miraculous substance was ever shown to witnesses. Indeed, we are not quite sure what the Stone was supposed to look like. It was often referred to as the Elixir or Tincture, an indication that it was a liquid, not a stone. It was not only credited with the power of transmutation, it was also said to cure all diseases, prolong life indefinitely, and accomplish a host of other miraculous things. The philosopher's stone was mankind's most magical object.

The primary reason why it is difficult to understand just exactly what the alchemist was after was that alchemy had a twofold nature; it was both practical and spiritual. The attempt to transmute base metals into gold was the practical side. In the Christian world, however, it was not possible to believe that the alchemist could succeed by human effort alone. The belief grew that the stone could only be made with the aid of divine grace and favor. Thus only the spiritually pure man could be a true alchemist. From this belief developed the system called hidden or esoteric alchemy which was concerned with the transformation of sinful man into the perfect being. The analogy of the transformation of "base" metal into "pure" gold was obvious. The two kinds of alchemy were thoroughly intertwined and often it is quite impossible to tell whether an alchemist is describing a physical experiment or a spiritual exercise. The stress on spiritual purity led to the paradoxical belief that, in order to make gold, a man must be pure enough not to want gold.

The belief in the spirits contained in matter led many alchemists to the conclusion that they could create an artificial man. This they called the homunculus. There were numerous methods proposed for creating this being. Here is one of them. The alchemist assembles various "needful" substances. Just exactly what substances are "needful" is, unfortunately, not specified. These substances are enclosed in a glass phial and buried in horse dung for forty days.

"At the end of this time, there will be something which will begin to move and live in the bottle. This something is a man, but a man who has no body and is transparent. Nevertheless, he exists, and nothing remains but to bring him up—which is not more difficult to do than to make him. You may accomplish it by daily feeding him—during forty weeks, and without extracting him from his dung hill—with the arcanum [secret spirit] of human blood. At the end of this time you shall have a veritable living child, having every member as well-proportioned as any infant born of a woman. He will only be much smaller than an ordinary child, and his physical education will require more care and attention."

Obscurity is the hallmark of all alchemical writings. In the first place, the alchemists really did not understand the physical transformations they were attempting to describe. They framed their descriptions in grand and poetic symbols. The alchemist might say that Sol or the Sun was devoured by the green dragon, whereas the modern chemist would describe the same process by saying that gold dissolves in the acid *aqua rega*. The alchemist's description is a lot prettier, but less concise. To the alchemist "the black crow" often meant lead, "the gray wolf" antimony, and "celestial dew" signified mercury or the "mercury principle." But the words did not mean the same thing to all alchemists, and the result was endless confusion. Often the alchemist abandoned words altogether, and used signs or symbolic drawings. Medieval alchemical art is often beautiful, and always strange.

The alchemist was also deliberately obscure. Many alchemists were simple fakers who promised to produce gold for a fee, and never delivered. They covered their ignorance with a flow of fancy words, meant to impress rather than inform. The alchemical confidence game worked time and again for centuries. Marie de Medici, consort of Henry IV of France, heard of an alchemist named Guy de Crusembourg who was imprisoned in the Bastille. She gave him twenty thousand crowns for his alchemical experiments, assuming that as a prisoner, he could find no other way of spending the money. Guy found a way. He escaped from the Bastille, and the Queen never saw him or her money again.

But the fakers were not always successful. An early eighteenth-

Two different views of the alchemist at work in his laboratory.

century imposter called Domenico Manuel Caetano had promised several German noblemen that he would prepare the philosopher's stone within sixty days, after the payment of a large fee. When no philosopher's stone was forthcoming the alchemist was dressed in a cloak covered with glittering tinsel, and hanged from a gilded gallows. The townsfolk even struck a medal to commemorate the occasion.

The honest alchemist felt an equally great need for hiding the results of his work. If he learned "the secret" then others might steal it from him. There was no such thing as a patent in those days. Hence, he sought to cover the progress of his work with vague and deliberately confusing descriptions. Most dangerous of all was the rumor that a particular alchemist actually possessed the philosopher's stone. One alchemist who also practiced medicine had effected some rather spectacular cures during an epidemic and the rumor got around that he had the Elixir. A mob, howling for the miraculous cure which he did not possess, descended upon his house and the terrified man had to sneak away in disguise. This alchemist said that he knew of many of his fellow alchemists who had been murdered because they were thought to possess the Stone, when in fact, they knew no more about it than their murderers.

The alchemical quest was the most compelling yet frustrating in history. Time after time alchemists reported being just at the point of distilling the essence, when the retort broke, or the crucible cracked, forcing them to start the laborious process all over again. In the late nineteenth century, the Rev. W. A. Ayton, an English clergyman and alchemist, claimed that he had actually prepared the Elixir and was just about to drink it when a long-winded visitor arrived. By the time the visitor had finished talking the volatile mixture had evaporated.

It is all too easy for us to laugh at the alchemists, and denounce them as fools for continuing the hopeless search for so many centuries. Why, we wonder, didn't they realize that they were on the wrong track? In fact, there was no greater percentage of fools among alchemists than among any other group. Some of the most intelligent men of their time had strong alchemical interests. Alchemy, like all other magical systems, is entirely self-confirming, once the basic propositions are accepted. As soon as people believed that there was a universal spirit, and that the preparation of the philosopher's stone was a theoretical possibility (and almost everybody believed this until the eighteenth century) then it seemed that the only problem was one of technique. If one didn't get the philosopher's stone it could only be because the experiments had not been performed properly. The experiments must, therefore, be done again, and perhaps next time, or the time after that, the desired end would finally be reached. In moments of discouragement the alchemist could always console himself with stories he had heard of a fellow seeker in some distant place who had discovered "the secret"—thus confirming his belief that his quest was a realistic one.

Many alchemists also believed that there was a secret society of adepts—who did hold the key to the mysteries. More than one faker made money by collecting "initiation fees" to such a nonexistent society from eager and gullible alchemists.

There was also a persistent tradition that the alchemical secrets were revealed in some ancient books and manuscripts, if only these works could be found and their strange symbols properly interpreted. The alchemist often became a frequenter of dusty bookstalls, and a collector of rare manuscripts.

The origins of alchemy are obscure. Much alchemical theory was based on the speculations of the early Greek natural philosophers about the universal spirit. The Arabs adopted the Greek alchemical tradition and through them it was transmitted to Western Europe in the later Middle Ages.

Though many magical practices were held suspect by the medieval Church, alchemy remained surprisingly respectable. Perhaps it was the alchemists' insistence on spiritual purity that allowed them to remain within the good graces of official Christianity.

Ultimately alchemy spawned chemistry and from the eighteenth century onward the work of the chemists began to destroy the theories upon which the search for the philosopher's stone had been based. Scientifically respectable alchemy disappeared long ago but the lure of the alchemical quest is strong, and in one form or another it continues to the present day, though at a considerably reduced level of activity.

A British alchemist named Archibald Cockrin who died in the 1960's claimed that he had made a crystal of gold grow like a plant. There was at least one frankly alchemical society operating in London in the 1960's. Other occult societies drop hints that they hold "the secret," and the symbolism of alchemy is still popular in the writings of today's occultists.

THE HERMETIC TRADITION

To the medieval alchemist the founder of his art was Hermes Trismegistus, a king or sage who lived in ancient Egypt. A vast body of alchemical and magical writings were attributed to this Hermes, and were enormously influential in Europe for several centuries. Alchemists often referred to their profession as the Hermetic Art.

Of all the Hermetic writings the most important was undoubtedly the Emerald Tablet.

According to tradition the Tablet was found in a cave. The words were etched in Phoenician characters on a slab of emerald clutched in the hands of the corpse of Hermes Trismegistus himself. The discoverer, in one version of the story, was Sara, the wife of Abraham, and the cave was located near Hebron. In other versions the tablet was found by Alexander the Great, or Apollonius of Tyana. Still another variation of the legend had Hermes giving the tablet to Miriam, the beautiful sister of Moses. The Arabs had Noah taking the Emerald Tablet with him on the Ark.

The Emerald Tablet was the work with which all good alchemists began their quest, and from it you can get a flavor of this important magical/alchemical tradition.

Hermes Trismegistus.

True it is, without falsehood, certain and most true. That which is above is like to that which is below, and that which is below is like to that which is above, to accomplish the miracles of one thing.

And as all things were by the contemplation of one, so all things arose from this one thing by a single act of adaptation.

The father thereof is the Sun, the mother the Moon.

The Wind carried in its womb, the Earth is nurse thereof.

It is the father of all works of wonder throughout the whole world.

The power thereof is perfect.

If it be cast onto Earth, it will separate the element of Earth from that of Fire, the subtle from the gross.

With great sagacity it doth ascend gently from Earth to Heaven.

Again it doth descend to Earth, and uniteth in itself the force from things superior and things inferior.

Thus thou wilt possess the glory of the brightness of the whole world, and all obscurity will fly far from thee.

This thing is the strong fortitude of all strength, for it overcometh every subtle thing and doth penetrate every solid substance.

Thus was the world created.

Hence there will be marvelous adaptations achieved, of which the manner is this.

For this reason I am called Hermes Trismegistus, because I hold three parts of the wisdom of the whole world.

That which I had to say about the operation of Sol is completed.

What does it all mean? No one really can say. The Emerald Tablet can be interpreted only in the most general way:

1. It is a statement of the basic magical belief of a correspondence or interaction between heavenly and earthly events. ("That which is above is like to that which is below")

2. Everything on heaven and earth has a single origin. ("So all things arose from this one thing")

3. The original "thing" seems to be sort of a living universal soul for the tablets speak of the "contemplation" and "adaptation" of the "one thing."

4. The possibility of transmutation is certainly implied. The sun and the moon mentioned in the tablet may be gold and silver; they usually were in alchemical writing.

Beyond these very general statements the meaning of the Emerald Tablet is shrouded in mystery and controversy. Many have tried to explain the Tablet, but the explanations were as hard to understand as the original. The Emerald Tablet certainly wasn't very practical as a guide for turning lead into gold, or preparing the elixir of life.

Unfortunately, the wonderful legends about the Hermetic writings have fallen before the researches of historians. In the seventeenth century, the real origins of the Hermetic books were discovered, helping to hasten the decline of interest in alchemy. They seem mostly to have been composed in Alexandria, Egypt, during the first few centuries of the Christian era. They are largely the products of the various heretical Christian sects which flourished at that time. These sects incorporated ancient magical lore and Greek natural philosophy into their doctrines. One of the things that had most impressed medieval scholars about the Hermetic writings is that though they were supposed to be pre-Christian, or even pre-Mosaic, there were numerous references to Christianity, which is perhaps why the Church itself looked with some kindness upon the Hermetic writings despite their unorthodoxy.

The famed Emerald Tablet may actually be older than the other Hermetic writings, though we cannot be sure. The first known account of it appears in a book written in Arabic during the ninth century. Scholars believe that the true origin of the Emerald Tablet was Greece or Syria, rather than the traditional homeland of mysteries, Egypt.

The effect of the Hermetic writings upon magical thought was twofold. First they established the popular magical idea that all things in the universe were somehow connected, and could influence one another. Second they reenforced the belief that the ancients had possessed great magical knowledge, and that this knowledge had been secretly passed on through the centuries by a small group of adepts, who had learned to master the obscure language of the ancient documents.

THE ROSICRUCIANS

How wonderful and exciting it would be to suddenly be initiated into an ancient secret society that held the key to "the Great Mysteries," be these alchemical, magical, or otherwise. For centuries men have dreamed that there was such a group, and even today those of

An alchemical drawing showing the resurrection of the adepts. Whether this resurrection is supposed to be physical or spiritual is unclear.

occult inclinations still search for such a secret society. The most common belief is that the wisdom of the ages is held by a mysterious brotherhood known as the Rosicrucians.

The first time anyone ever seems to have heard of the Rosicrucians was in 1614. A pamphlet describing the origins of the mysterious brotherhood was circulated anonymously in the town of Cassel, Germany. It told of the life of a man identified only as C.R.C. (later documents asserted that C.R.C. was Christianus Rosae Crucis, or more popularly Christian Rosenkreuz). Rosenkreuz was supposed to have been born in 1378, and while still a boy he set out on a pilgrimage to Jerusalem. Somehow he was sidetracked and wound up wandering all through the Middle East learning various occult secrets.

After years of wandering he returned to Germany where, with the aid of eight monks, he founded a secret order called the Fraternity of the Rosy Cross or the Rosicrucians. The members of this order were to disperse throughout Europe, and using their occult knowledge, subtly influence the course of events. All members were sworn to absolute secrecy, and each member named his own successor before he died. A somewhat later tradition held that the Rosicrucians tried to perpetuate their order by producing the homunculas.

Rosenkreuz, the documents asserted, lived on to the age of 106 and then was buried in a secret tomb. Over the door of the tomb were the words, "I shall open after 120 years."

Thus in the year 1604 the doors to the tomb sprung open, and the members of the order viewed the marvelous seven-sided vault which held the body of their founder. The interior of the vault was illuminated by an ever-burning light, and they viewed the body of Rosenkreuz himself, miraculously uncorrupted despite its 120 years of burial. Surrounding the body was a variety of magical objects, and clutched in the hands was a document called "Book T" which was described as "our greatest treasure next to the Bible."

The opening of the tomb door signaled at least a partial end of secrecy for the order. They now offered membership to all worthy individuals. But joining the Rosicrucians turned out to be a don't-call-us-we'll-call-you proposition. The prospective initiate was supposed to make his interest in the society known to the public, and then wait to be contacted. Some persons announced their interest and waited, but as far as can be determined, none was ever contacted.

The following year a second document attributed to the mysterious group was published in Cassel, but the authors remained as unknown as ever. The year after that the strangest of the original Rosicrucian documents appeared. It was called *The Chemical Wedding of Christian Rosenkreuz.* Both of the earlier documents had denounced alchemy, though they used alchemical symbolism, but this third document, as the title implies, was virtually an alchemical treatise. The book describes the marriage of a mythical king and queen, at a ceremony in which Rosenkreuz is the guest of honor. But before he reaches the ceremony, Rosenkreuz is forced to undergo many bizarre ordeals. This was typical alchemical allegory—the ordeals were the purification of the soul, or perhaps the purification of matter. On the one hand the authors of the Rosicrucian documents claimed to possess more gold and silver than anyone in the world; on the other, they sneered at the mere search for riches, and indicated that the true goal of the society was the regeneration of the soul.

There is considerable doubt that there ever really was any sort of Rosicrucian society. The best guess today is that the whole idea was dreamed up by a group of university students interested in Hermetic magic and Christian mysticism. The leader of the group was probably Johann Andrea (1586–1654). Andrea actually admitted writing the *Chemical Wedding*, and significantly the Rose and Cross, symbols of the alleged society, were also part of the coat of arms of Andrea's family. Perhaps Andrea and his friends really did wish to start such a society, and perhaps it was all an elaborate joke. We shall never know.

Whatever the origin, societies bearing the Rosicrucian name began to appear in many places. In August, 1623, these notices were supposedly posted in Paris:

"We deputies of the principal college of the Brethren of the Rosy Cross, are staying visibly and invisibly in this town by the Grace of the Most High, to whom the heart of the Just turns. We show and teach without books or masks how to speak the language of every country where we wish to be, to bring our fellow men out of the error of death."

The first person to apply for fellowship in the Order, so the story goes, was a lawyer who was heavily in debt. He wanted to find out the secret of becoming invisible, so that his creditors could not locate him. He finally succeeded in finding the elusive brothers, and they agreed to teach him their secrets. But they all ate and drank so well before the initiation that when the lawyer was to be baptized by immersion in the river, he drowned.

A typical medieval alchemical drawing. The drawing is filled with symbols, only some of which can be understood. The alchemist and his guiding spirit are shown praying beside the alchemical furnace. At top two angels hold a vessel containing the symbols Neptune (water), Sol (gold), and Luna (silver), beneath the Sun.

The most extensive defense of the Rosicrucians was written in 1618 by a German physician and philosopher named Michael Maier. According to Maier the society was successor to a series of secret groups including the Magi of Persia and Egypt. He said that the Rosicrucians must be judged by the few true adepts rather than by the host of imposters and charlatans who had appropriated the name.

What were the secrets possessed by the Rosicrucians? According to Maier the true adepts possessed a wisdom consisting of a mastery of religion; of medicine; of "natural magic"; of the "perfection of all arts"; of alchemy; and of the "anatomy and idea of the whole universe." Their ultimate secret was that of "incredible virtue," which ensured that piety, justice, and truth prevailed in their characters and that the contrary vices were dispelled. Though Maier's book is very long, there is much he does not say. He never discusses exactly what Rosicrucian magic or art was. Maier himself was not a member of the fraternity, and perhaps he didn't know. But no true Rosicrucian adept ever seems to have written about the activities of his society.

Over the years Rosicrucian societies have come and gone. Each society claims that it, and it alone, is the true Rosicrucian society, and that all others are fraudulent. Since there is no evidence that there ever was an original Rosicrucian society, the claims of one group are quite as good as those of the next.

Today the alchemical emphasis of early Rosicrucianism is largely forgotten, because alchemy is no longer popular. Yet it has not disappeared entirely. In 1916 H. Spencer Lewis, founder of the popular American mail-order Rosicrucian society, the Ancient Mystical Order Rosae Crucis (AMORC) claimed that he had transmuted a piece of zinc into gold. But rather than using the traditional apparatus of the alchemist, he said he used "a little known power of the mind."

NICOLAS FLAMEL

The story of Nicolas Flamel inspired generations of alchemists. Not only was Flamel one of those who had reputedly found the secret of transmuting base metals into gold, he was a real nice guy as well.

Flamel was born near Paris around the year 1330. He was trained as a public scribe or notary. In those preprinting days the position of scribe was an important one. Flamel and his assistants copied documents and manuscripts, and branched out into the business of teaching rich people how to write. All this produced a comfortable income which became more comfortable when the scribe married a wealthy widow. But Nicolas Flamel was no fortune hunter; he always spoke of his wife, Pernelle, with the greatest affection. The couple lived together, simply and frugally, despite their not inconsiderable wealth. Theirs seems to have been a happy marriage.

Many alchemical manuscripts must have passed through the hands of the scribe, but he had no interest in the subject until one night when he had a strange dream. An angel appeared holding a book and said, "Flamel, look at this book. You will not in the least understand it, neither will anyone else; but a day will come when you will see in it something that no one else will see." As Flamel stretched out his hand to take the book, both angel and book dissolved in a cloud of gold.

Then sometime later, in the year 1357, Flamel found in the collection of an unknown manuscript vendor, the very book about which he had dreamed.

There fell into my hands, for the sum of two florins, a gilded book, very old and large; it was not of paper or parchment, as other books are, but made only of thin bark (as it seemed to me) of tender shrubs. Its cover was of copper, very delicate, and engraved all over with strange letters or figures. I could not read them but I thought they might be in Greek or some other ancient language. The leaves of bark inside were covered with beautiful and very clear Latin letters, which had been inscribed with a steel point and coloured. The book contained three times seven leaves, for so they were numbered at the top of the leaves, the seventh leaf always without writing on it, but instead, on the first seventh leaf, had been painted a rod with two serpents swallowing one another; on the second seventh, a cross on which a serpent was crucified; and on the last seventh were painted deserts, in the midst of which ran beautiful fountains, from whence there issued many serpents which ran hither and thither. Upon the first of the leaves there was

Nicolas Flamel.

written, in large capital letters of gold: ABRAHAM THE JEW, PRINCE, LEVIT, ASTROLOGER, AND PHILOSOPHER TO THE NATION OF THE JEWS, BY THE WRATH OF GOD DISPERSED AMONG THE GAULS SENDETH SALUTATION. After this it was filled with great execrations and curses . . . against every person that should cast his eyes upon it, unless he were Sacrificer or Scribe.

As a scribe, Flamel felt exempted from the curses. A careful examination of the text indicated that it was indeed alchemical. Apparently it contained the formula used by the Jews to make gold to pay the tribute due the Roman Empire. But some of the pages contained pictures without any text. These Flamel guessed held the secret to the philosopher's stone, but the scribe could make nothing of them.

Flamel kept the book a secret from everyone but his faithful Pernelle. He pored over it by the hour, but the more he studied the less he seemed to understand. Flamel then began discreetly showing copies of some of the drawings to local alchemists. On the basis of what the alchemists told him he began his own experiments. These continued for twenty-one years without success. The patient Nicolas Flamel was finally getting discouraged, when he suddenly hit upon a bright idea. Since the book had been prepared by Abraham the Jew, then perhaps it would take a Jew to understand it.

At that time Spain had a large number of Jewish scholars. Flamel decided to make a pilgrimage to St. James of Compostella, near Corunna in Spain. He hoped by this pious act, God would guide him to some learned Jew who could interpret the manuscript. The pilgrimage was accomplished without incident, but after spending nearly a year frequenting Spanish synagogues, Flamel found no one who could help him. On his return journey, however, he was introduced to a converted Jew named Maître Canches, a scholar of the cabala (the cabala is a book of Jewish mysticism and magic and figures importantly in some alchemical speculation). Maître Canches recognized Flamel's copies as coming from the *Asch Mezareph* of the Rabbi Abraham. This was a book cabalists thought had been lost forever. Maître Canches deciphered the drawings for Flamel, in a way quite different from that of the traditional alchemist. He also asked to accompany Flamel to Paris so he could look at the original volume, but he died on the way. Still, when Flamel reached home again he was happy, for he felt that he now possessed enough of the secret to work out the rest by himself.

Three more years of hard work lay ahead of him. His efforts were crowned with success on Monday, January 17, 1382, when with the white Elixir he and Pernelle changed half a pound of lead into pure silver. He then went ahead to prepare the red or Great Elixir.

"And then, following my book word for word, I made projection of the Red Stone upon half a pound of mercury, in the presence of Pernelle only, in the same house, the five-and-twentieth day of April following, the same year, about five o'clock in the evening; which I transmuted truly into about the same quantity of pure gold, most certainly better than ordinary gold, being more soft and pliable."

Flamel wasn't greedy; he only accomplished this transmutation two more times in his life, and he continued to live in the same frugal, pious manner as before.

Pernelle died in 1397. For a time Flamel was inconsolable, but he managed to recover himself, and spent the remaining years of his life writing about alchemy and doing good works. When he died on March 22, 1417, he left behind a notable record of endowments to churches, hospitals, and other charitable institutions.

Though Flamel had been a highly respected man while he lived, after his death his neighbors believed that a piece of the philosopher's stone might still be hidden somewhere. They ransacked his property, literally tearing down some of the buildings, stone by stone. Nearly two centuries later, the hope of finding Flamel's secret hidden somewhere led a local magistrate to take possession of all the property that formerly belonged to the alchemist and order that a thorough search be made. Nothing was ever found.

Did Nicolas Flamel really possess the secret of transmuting base metals into gold? For centuries alchemists thought so, and apparently

Flamel himself believed that he did. His contemporaries pointed to the large fortune that he left, as proof that he could make gold. Yet the fortune, though considerable, is not beyond what might have been accumulated by a successful but frugal scribe, with a rich wife.

That both Flamel and his wife actually died, there is no doubt. His tombstone has been found, as has her extremely detailed will. Yet there is a tradition that in addition to transmuting gold the alchemist also made the elixir of life and he and his wife attained immortality. They were reportedly seen alive and well in India in the seventeenth century. In the mid-eighteenth century a number of people testified that the pair had attended the opera in Paris. However, they have not been heard from recently.

PARACELSUS

The high point of alchemy was reached in the career of that strange and quarrelsome genius who called himself Paracelsus. The name he chose was a key to his character. It meant greater than Celsus, a Roman physician whose writings on medicine were considered almost gospel by physicians of the Middle Ages.

Paracelsus, or to give his proper name, Theophrastus Bombastus von Hohenheim, was born near Zurich, Switzerland, on December 17, 1493. His father was a physician and possibly an alchemist. We have only a spotty knowledge of Paracelsus' early life. He traveled a great deal, probably serving as an army surgeon in various campaigns. He turned up in Italy long enough to earn a medical degree at the University of Ferrara. As he traveled, Paracelsus was willing to learn from everybody—physicians, alchemists, astrologers, apothecaries, miners, gypsies, and adepts at various occult arts. When he finally settled in Germany near the Swiss border in 1526 he possessed an unparalleled fund of odd and curious knowledge.

In that year he had a stroke of luck. Johann Froben, a prosperous publisher in Basel, fell ill and none of the local physicians was able to cure him. Paracelsus was sent for and effected a quick and complete

Paracelsus.

cure. Froben happened to be a friend of many of northern Europe's greatest scholars, and they helped to spread the fame of the new physician. He was appointed to the position of city physician for Basel, and made a professor of medicine.

Though his skills as a physician were considerable, Paracelsus certainly did not have the personality to hold public office. Aside from his all too apparent egomania he was also a drunk, "marvelous Paracelsus, always drunk and always lucid." Worse still he had one of the quickest tempers and foulest mouths in history.

He began his public career by ostentatiously burning all of the classical texts on medicine. To his fellow physicians he proclaimed, "O you hypocrites, who despise the truths taught you by a great physician, who is himself instructed by Nature, and is a son of God himself! Come then, and listen imposters . . . Woe for your necks in the day of judgement! I know that the monarchy will be mine. Mine too, will be the honor and the glory. Not that I praise myself: Nature praises me. . . ."

After he got through assailing physicians in general he began reviling them as individuals. "You wormy and lousy Sophist . . ." was one of his milder insults. Unsurprisingly all of the physicians and apothecaries of Basel were soon agitating to get rid of their tormentor. But the city fathers stuck by their alarming prodigy. Within a few months, however, Paracelsus was in court suing a rich patient for nonpayment. When the case unexpectedly went against him he unleashed a flow of such unprecedented epithets at the horrified magistrates that he left himself open for severe punishment for contempt of court. Paracelsus then departed from Basel quietly and in a hurry.

For a while he wandered about mostly in Germany. His luck had entirely deserted him and, dressed in rags, he resembled a tramp more than a physician. Paracelsus was finally invited to the court of the Archbishop Duke Ernst of Bavaria, a keen student of occultism. Worn out by a lifetime of quarreling, drinking, and traveling, Paracelsus died at the court of his new patron in April, 1541. Like Agrippa, he was only forty-eight years old when he died.

Paracelsus wrote a number of books, and many others were written by his followers and attributed to him. This body of work was to have a great influence on magical thinkers of later times, as well as having some influence on the sciences of medicine and chemistry.

As an alchemist Paracelsus was not interested in the transmutation of lead into gold, though he did not deny that such a change was possible. "Many have said of alchemy that it is for making gold and silver. For me such is not the aim, but to consider only what virtue and power may lie in medicines."

In the Paracelsan view of the world, all health and illness were controlled by the heavens. The job of the alchemist was to prepare an "arcana" or secret remedy which would restore the celestial harmony between the human body and the stars. The healing power of the arcana was the spirit it contained, not the substance itself, though much effort had to go into the preparation of the material arcana to insure that it contained the correct spirit. Such an outlook fitted right into the magical tradition.

In denouncing the subservience of his fellow physicians to the medical writings of the ancients, Paracelsus helped to free medicine from the dead weight of the past. His violent diatribes against apothecaries who failed to take the proper care in making their preparations doubtless had some effect. Paracelsus introduced into medicine opium, mercury, and compounds of antimony, and was the first to study anesthesia induced by ether. But in the end, the cures that Paracelsus was able to offer his patients were really not much better than those offered by other physicians of the day, and that is to say not very good at all.

It was Paracelsus' occult ideas, concerning the universal spirit and the interactions of the planets upon man, that were most influential. The magically inclined of future generations were to study his works carefully, and elevate him to the position of a demigod. Many said he had successfully created the artificial man called the homunculus.

Paracelsus' writings are like those of other alchemists; they are open to a variety of interpretations since he is deliberately obscure. He said that he could condense all the alchemical knowledge in the world into ten books, but that he would write only nine of them. The tenth, which would provide the key to the rest, would remain unwritten until the world recanted of its errors "and promised perfect submission to Paracelsus." The world didn't recant, but Paracelsus wrote the tenth book anyway. In a way he kept his word, because he didn't give away any secrets. One occultist has described this book as "a key which could pass for a lock, and for a lock which we cannot even pick."

6
MAGIC IN THE AGE OF REASON

THE EIGHTEENTH CENTURY

BY THE EIGHTEENTH CENTURY magic was really in trouble. In the villages, and among the poor in the cities, the cunning men and women operated as they always had. But among the educated, magic had begun to lose its respectability. It wasn't just that the pretensions of this or that magician were denounced as fraudulent and foolish; that sort of criticism had always existed. Now the whole system of magical thinking was under attack. Science and the scientific method began to fill some of the intellectual and emotional needs that were once filled by magic. Educated men and women read, or tried to read, the works of scientists like Isaac Newton rather than Agrippa, and instead of alchemy they experimented with physics and chemistry. Man was turning from an animistic view of the universe to a mechanistic one, in which nature was governed by mathematical laws, which could not be gotten round by a charm or spell.

Yet that was only one side of the picture. A mechanistic universe is cold, unsatisfying, and impersonal. In the new world of science and reason, religion itself was under attack and no longer offered men the comfort it had in the past. The magicians still appealed to some of the deeper and unsatisfied human needs for reassurance, for the appearance of power, for excitement, and for mystery. Though the magician no longer commanded the unquestioned respect he once possessed, magic still attracted many from among the wealthy and educated. It was said, with some justification, that the eighteenth century was skeptical of everything but occultism. This paradox was greatest in France, home of Voltaire, Diderot, and most of the other skeptical intellectuals of the Enlightenment. But eighteenth-century France was also the stage which held two of the most colorful magical figures in history, Saint-Germain and Cagliostro. France was also the center for the semimagical cult that formed around the teachings of Franz Mesmer.

SAINT-GERMAIN

The Comte de Saint-Germain never claimed that he possessed the elixir of life, or that he had already lived several hundred years, but if others chose to believe such stories, he did not contradict them.

No one really knows who Saint-Germain was, though we can be fairly certain that his name was not Saint-Germain and that he was not a count. The best guess is that he was a Portuguese Jew and that he was born around the year 1710.

Nothing at all is known of his early life. Around the year 1740 he seems to have been arrested in London as a spy. Somewhat later he turned up in Germany selling his elixir. A French aristocrat, visiting Germany, induced Saint-Germain to settle in Paris around 1748.

Saint-Germain was a man of great charm and persuasiveness. He became a popular figure at the gatherings of the rich and well-born. Quite soon the most incredible stories about him began to make the rounds of Parisian society. At one dinner party, so it was said, Saint-Germain was speaking with easy familiarity of King Richard the

Lion-Hearted, and some of the conversations they had while in Palestine together during the Crusades. When some of the other guests were openly skeptical, Saint-Germain turned to his valet, who was standing behind his chair, and asked him to confirm the truth of the story.

"I really cannot say, sir," the servant replied. "You forget, sir, I have only been five hundred years in your service!"

"Ah! True," said Saint-Germain. "I remember now—it was a little before your time!"

On one occasion the king's mistress, Madame de Pompadour, complained, "But you do not tell us your age, and yet you pretend you are very old. The Countess de Gergy, who was, I believe, ambassadress at Vienna some fifty years ago, says she saw you there exactly the same as you now appear."

"It is true, Madame," replied Saint-Germain. "I knew Madame de Gergy many years ago."

"But according to her account, you must be more than a hundred years old?"

"That is not impossible, but it is much more possible that the good lady is in her dotage."

When Pompadour pressed Saint-Germain to give the king some of his celebrated elixir he replied, "Oh, Madame, the physicians would have me broken on the wheel, were I to think of drugging his majesty."

Saint-Germain treated his reputation for great wealth the same way he treated his reputation for great age—he made no specific claims, but if people chose to believe that he possessed the alchemical secret of transmuting gold, or of making precious stones out of ordinary ones, he would not deny it.

Once he showed Pompadour and her ladies a great quantity of sparkling stones. Pompadour's practiced eye was quick to observe that almost all of the flashy stones were fakes. But amid this collection of paste jewels he displayed a superb genuine ruby. He also produced a small jeweled cross, of good workmanship but moderate value. When one of Pompadour's ladies expressed admiration for the little cross, Saint-Germain presented it to her, professing to disdain all wealth. So it seems, by a clever mixture of real and false jewels, Saint-Germain managed to sustain his reputation for limitless wealth. How he really did make his money is something of a mystery. He may have made some by selling his elixir of life. Some may have come from his activities as a spy. Mostly though, it appears he lived off the generosity of his many wealthy friends.

Around the year 1760, Saint-Germain left Paris, for political reasons some said. From that time onwards, stories of his comings and goings are vague and unreliable. It was rumored that he was in London, in St. Petersburg, and in Germany. He seems to have spent his final days at the court of his friend, the Prince of Hesse-Cassel, dying there in the year 1782.

What was the Comte de Saint-Germain? Many believe he was nothing more than a charming and clever fraud. Even occultists who revere his memory admit that there was much of the actor about him. Yet his life was so shrouded in mystery that there is still room for doubt. His true identity remains unknown to this day. The date of his

The Comte de Saint-Germain.

birth is completely unknown, and the date of his death is at best uncertain. There were those who claimed, and still claim, that Saint-Germain never died. From time to time during the past two centuries people have turned up saying that they have met Saint-Germain, or that they actually were Saint-Germain. Most commonly it is claimed that Saint-Germain has entered that vague world of semidivine and immortal masters or adepts.

Perhaps the most recent "meeting" with Saint-Germain took place in the 1920's on the top of Mt. Shasta in northern California. The man who claimed that he had come face to face with the undying Saint-Germain was a Kansas born spirit medium and occultist named Guy Warren Ballard. According to Ballard Saint-Germain imparted certain secrets to him, and on the basis of these secrets Ballard and his wife organized the I AM movement, which had thousands of followers during the 1920's and 30's.

In their churches the Ballards had two pictures on the wall: one of Jesus and the other showing a bearded and robed individual identified as Saint-Germain. In fact, the pictures of Saint-Germain made during his lifetime show him as beardless, bewigged, and dressed in the most fashionable clothes of his day.

The Ballards had strong fascistic leanings, and they organized a little body of private storm troopers called the Minute Men of Saint-Germain. They also said that they could destroy their enemies by blasting them with "Saint-Germain's Blue Ray." During the ceremonies of the I AM cult members sat around thinking about their enemies and shouting "Blast! Blast! Blast!" in unison. As far as we know, no one was ever hurt by "Saint-Germain's Blue Ray," and the I AM cult itself petered out during World War II, when its founder's pro-Nazi sympathies made them extremely unpopular. Still, the fact that twentieth-century occultists would name the eighteenth-century Saint-Germain as "Chief of the Ascended Masters" will give some idea of how important he is in occult and magical history.

Skeptics say that the real Saint-Germain was secretive because he was a fraud. Occultists say he was secretive because there was much he could not reveal to the world. They contend that he deliberately ridiculed his own powers in order to throw people off the track. But, say the occultists, he revealed his secrets to a small number of selected followers. During his stay in Paris secret societies, such as the Rosicrucians, were popular. These societies often employed Hermetic and cabalistic symbols and many of the rituals common to high magic. Whether Saint-Germain himself ever belonged to any such society we cannot say for sure, but it is not unlikely. Saint-Germain's successor and imitator Count Allendro de Cagliostro said that Saint-Germain had been the founder of Freemasonry, another secret society, in France, and that Saint-Germain had personally initiated Cagliostro and his wife at his Temple of Mystery.

There are several accounts of this initiation ceremony. They differ in detail, but all contain descriptions of various tests and trials similar to those attributed to the ancient Magi, as well as of the long-winded speeches about truth and mystery which seem an inevitable part of initiation ceremonies of secret societies. According to a book called *Lives of the Alchemical Philosophers*, after the trials were successfully completed, Saint-Germain passed on to his new followers the "great secret" of his society. The "secret" was that Saint-Germain and his elixir were fakes.

"Several essential precepts were enjoined upon them, among others that they must detest, avoid and calumniate men of understanding, but flatter, foster, and blind, fools; that they must spread abroad with much mystery and intelligence that the Comte de Saint-Germain was five hundred years old, and that they must make gold, but dupes before all."

Enemies of secret societies often alleged that the only real "secrets" of such groups were that there was no secret, and that the only aim of all the magical or religious ritual was to impress and confuse the foolish. It was said of the Assassins, most famous of the Moslem secret societies, that those who reached the top grade were told this great secret, "Nothing is true, everything is permitted."

Is a philosophy like this the secret of Saint-Germain? Like everything else about the man, this too is a mystery. Saint-Germain has taken the answer to the question with him to the grave, or wherever else he may happen to be at this moment.

CAGLIOSTRO

The man who called himself the Count Allendro de Cagliostro and who has been described by some as "one of the greatest occult figures of all time," was described by others as "the archquack of his age, the last of the great pretenders to the philosopher's stone and the water of life."

Most people today believe Cagliostro's real name was Joseph Balsamo, and he was born in Palermo, Sicily, in about 1743. His family was poor, and at the age of fifteen he was sent to a monastery for an education. There he proved to be a mean and unruly pupil, being implicated in numerous robberies and several murders, including the murder of an uncle who had befriended him.

During his disreputable youth, Balsamo picked up some knowledge of the forms of magic and alchemy. He used this knowledge in Palermo to swindle a superstitious goldsmith named Marano out of sixty ounces of gold. When Marano found that he had been duped, instead of going directly to the police he swore a vendetta against Balsamo, vowing to kill him at the first convenient opportunity. Balsamo took the threat seriously and departed for Arabia forthwith.

At the city of Medina, Balsamo met a mysterious Greek named Althotas, who was dressed as an Oriental chieftain and was always accompanied by an Albanian greyhound. Balsamo, who by this time was calling himself Count Cagliostro, among other aliases, fell into conversation with the stranger and arranged to visit him at his house. He was told to call "a little before midnight, and to rap twice on the knocker, then three times more slowly when he would be admitted. At the appointed time Cagliostro duly appeared and was conducted along a narrow passage lit by a single lamp in a niche of the wall. At the end of this was a spacious apartment illuminated by wax candles, and furnished with everything necessary for the practice of alchemy."

Althotas proposed that Cagliostro accompany him to Egypt and when Cagliostro inquired as to who was going to pay for the journey, Althotas waved his hand and indicated that obtaining gold was no problem for him. So off they went to Egypt, where according to Cagliostro's later testimony:

> I inspected these celebrated pyramids which to the eye of the superficial observer only appear an enormous mass of marble and granite. I also got acquainted with the priests of the various temples, who had the complacence to introduce me into such places as no ordinary traveller ever entered before. The next three years of my progress were spent in the principal kingdoms of Africa and Asia. Accompanied by Althotas, and three attendants who continued in my service, I arrived in 1766 at the island of Rhodes, and there embarked on a French ship bound to Malta.

At Malta the travelers were warmly received by Pinto, the grand master of the Knights of Malta and a famous alchemist in his own right. But Cagliostro was an incurable wanderer who soon tired of puttering about an alchemical laboratory, and left for Italy carrying valuable letters of introduction from the grand master. According to some accounts he opened a gambling casino while others assert he supported himself as an alchemist and fortune-teller.

At about this time he met and married Lorenza Feliciana, the intelligent and beautiful daughter of a bankrupt noble family. She also possessed "the least principle of any of the maidens in Rome," so said Cagliostro's enemies.

The Count and Countess de Cagliostro, as the couple styled themselves, traveled throughout Europe telling fortunes, selling alchemical secrets, raising spirits, and doing whatever else itinerant magicians must do to make a living. In London, Cagliostro claimed that he knew the secret of picking winning lottery tickets. But the people to whom he tried to sell this "secret" were swindlers and everyone involved in the scheme very nearly wound up in jail. The count and countess were forced to move on.

Lorenza was arrested in Paris, reputedly on Cagliostro's complaint, when she tried to run off with another man. After a few months in jail, Lorenza was reconciled with her husband. Cagliostro then had the poor judgment to go to Palermo where he was immediately arrested on a charge brought by his old enemy the goldsmith Marano, but friends procured his release.

Up to this point Cagliostro was basically selling alchemy and fortune-telling and business was poor, for both of these practices were fast losing whatever respectability they once had. Indeed, Cagliostro was probably the last really well-known alchemist. But it is not his alchemical claims that made Cagliostro important in the history of magic. His true fame comes from the occult and magical influences he tried to bring to the movement of Freemasonry.

In Protestant England where Freemasonry began, the secret society was relatively noncontroversial and even respectable. Besides it wasn't very secret; everybody knew who the Masons were and what they stood for.

Despite all the elaborate ritual, the original Order of Freemasons was a rather modest group. It was an organization of men who basically liked to engage in speculative discussions about the nature of man and of the universe. Often these discussions involved magic or magical theory, but the original Masons made no hard and fast claims to supernatural knowledge as had the Rosicrucians. So many rich and aristocratic individuals joined the Order that it became the "thing" to join, even if one was not interested in speculative discussion.

In Catholic France the Freemasons faced a different situation. The Freemasons, while tolerant of most beliefs, were basically anti-Catholic. In return the Roman Catholic clergy hated the Freemasons with a passion, and in Catholic countries the Order had to be genuinely secretive. Under these circumstances it often assumed exotic forms. The most exotic was Egyptian Freemasonry, introduced (or invented) by Cagliostro.

Cagliostro was supposed to have come to know of this particular brand of Masonry after finding a "curious manuscript" in a London bookstall. The document dealt with the mysteries of Egyptian Masonry, and abounded with magical and mystical references. Cagliostro also had his meeting with Saint-Germain at this time, though whether this took place in London or elsewhere is uncertain.

What was Egyptian Freemasonry? The question is not easy to answer because its rites, as always, were "secret" and many scandalous, though unsupported, stories were spread about it. Two things are known: first, people of all religions and women were admitted to the society, whereas most secret societies had been limited to Protestant males. The women's section was presided over by Lorenza, Cagliostro's wife. Second, the initiation fee was high and probably helped support Cagliostro and Lorenza in the opulent life-style which they craved.

The final act of the initiation of women into Egyptian Masonry was supposed to come when the ceiling of the vaulted chamber opened, and a sphere of gold was lowered into the room. On the sphere sat

Cagliostro.

"The Grand Copt" Cagliostro, "naked as the unfallen Adam, holding a serpent in his hand, and having a burning star upon his head."

He welcomed the women into the society, and said that he was going to reveal to them the secrets of the ages. "The Grand Copt thereupon commanded them to dispense with the profanity of clothing, for if they would receive the truth they must be as naked as itself." He then launched into a long harangue about how magic was going to bring material prosperity and spiritual peace back to mankind. When he was finished he climbed back on his golden sphere and was pulled up through the ceiling.

According to Cagliostro, the secrets of Egyptian Freemasonry had first been revealed to the biblical prophets Enoch and Elias, but the system had been much debased until he rediscovered its original secrets. Cagliostro promised that those who became disciples of his society would be led to perfection by means of physical and moral regeneration. They would be returned to that state of perpetual youth, beauty, and innocence of which mankind had been deprived by original sin.

Cagliostro's formula for eternal life was a mixture of magic and the medical theories of the day:

> . . . retire into the country in the month of May, and during forty days . . . live according to the most strict and austere rules, eating very little, and then only laxative and sanative herbs, making use of no other drink than distilled water, or rain that has fallen in the course of the month. On the seventeenth day, after having let blood, certain white drops are to be taken six at night and six in the morning, increasing them two a day in progression. In three days more a small quantity of blood is again let from the arm before sunrise, and the patient is to retire to bed till the operation is completed. A grain of the panacea is then to be taken; this panacea is the same as that with which God created man when He made him immortal. When this is swallowed the candidate loses his speech and his reflection for three entire days and is subject to frequent convulsions, struggles, and perspirations. Having recovered from this state, in which however, he experiences no pain whatever, on that day he takes the third and last grain of the panacea, which

causes him to fall into a profound and tranquil sleep; it is then that he loses his hair, his skin, and his teeth. These are all reproduced in a few hours, and having become a new man on the morning of the fortieth day he leaves his room, enjoying a complete rejuvenescence, by which he is enabled to live 5557 years, or to such time as he, of his own accord, may be desirous of going to the world of the spirits.

While Cagliostro was riding high in public favor in Paris, he was implicated in a complex plot designed to steal a diamond necklace under the guise that it was being purchased by Queen Marie Antoinette. By introducing the queen's name into the affair the crime had immediately become one of great public interest. The real perpetrator of the crime, a certain Countess de Lamotte, accused Cagliostro and his wife of stealing the necklace, and the pair, along with the several others who had been named by the countess, spent months in the Bastille before coming to trial.

Flamboyant, even in the face of grave danger, Cagliostro delivered a resounding defense of himself:

> I am oppressed! I am accused! I am calumniated! Have I deserved this fate? I probe my conscience; and there I find the peace which men deny me! I have traveled a great deal. I am known all over Europe, and throughout a great part of Asia and Africa. I have everywhere shown myself as the friend of my fellow creatures. My knowledge, my time, my fortune have been employed in the relief of distress.

On and on he went, proclaiming his own selfless and saintly nature and giving a highly colored account of his own life. It is doubtful if the court believed a word of it. But there was really no evidence against Cagliostro and his wife so they were acquitted of the charge of stealing the necklace. But they were also banished from France and forced to leave most of the wealth that they had accumulated behind. Fleeing to England, Cagliostro is supposed to have angrily predicted the French Revolution and the doom of all those who had opposed him.

According to a story attributed to the French occultist Court de Gebelin, Cagliostro translated the names of the king and queen of France into the language of the ancient Magi. Then using the methods of Pythagorean numerology he was able to trace their fates, and he foretold that both would die on the scaffold, at the hands of revolutionaries. When Cagliostro's friends implored him to warn the royal couple, Cagliostro said that they would not believe him, and besides there was no way to change a predestined fate.

"All your protests will not prevent Predestination from being a fact and the Name a sign to be feared. The highest wisdom of the ancients believed in this mysterious connection of the name and the being who holds it. . . ."

Cagliostro's reputation began to evaporate once he was publicly identified as Joseph Balsamo, the swindler of Palermo. He and his wife wandered from place to place, finally going to Rome—a fatal mistake as it turned out.

When Cagliostro tried to start a lodge of his Egyptian Freemasons society in Rome he was immediately arrested. Masonry was an anathema to the Roman Catholic church, and to attempt to practice it at the very heart of the Papal States was an act of rashness that bordered upon the insane. Cagliostro was charged with being a Freemason, a heretic, and a sorcerer. After an examination by the Holy Inquisition he was condemned to death on April 7, 1791. Lorenza was also arrested, but allowed to live on the condition that she "confess" and enter a convent. Ultimately Cagliostro's death sentence was commuted by the pope to a sentence of perpetual imprisonment in the Castle of Saint Angelo. After an unsuccessful escape attempt he was moved to the fortress of San Leo, where he was placed in a tiny rock-cut dungeon until he died in 1795.

There were inevitably those who claimed that Cagliostro had not died in prison but had actually escaped. Others said that as the possessor of the secret of eternal life he could not die. In some occult philosophies, Cagliostro is another of the immortal, semidivine adepts. Still other occultists, Aleister Crowley for example, claimed to be reincarnations of Cagliostro.

In 1910 a biographer of Cagliostro stated that the identification of the "Count" with Joseph Balsamo was false, based only on unsupported circumstantial evidence and Cagliostro's confession that was extracted from him by the threat of torture. That is the view that many occultists still hold today.

What of Cagliostro's secrets? If they ever existed they seem to have done him little good in life, and were lost after his death.

FRANZ MESMER

In the decade of the 1780's all Paris was alive with talk of the almost miraculous cures being performed daily by an Austrian physician named Franz Anton Mesmer. Orthodox physicians denounced Mesmer as a charlatan while his numerous admirers hailed him as the founder of a whole new era of medical treatment. In a way both admirers and detractors were right, for in the career of Franz Mesmer science and magic were thoroughly intertwined.

Mesmer was born in Austria in 1734. At school he studied a number of subjects in a rather leisurely fashion, until he finally earned a degree in medicine from the University of Vienna. Mesmer's thesis was written on the subject of "The Influence of the Planets on the Human Body." The thesis was neither original nor startling. It was based largely on the theories of Paracelsus that there was a universal force or spirit that affected every object in the universe. Though this idea was not generally accepted in the early eighteenth century, it did not sound as strange then as it does today.

For some years after his graduation, Mesmer practiced orthodox medicine in Vienna. Then he became interested in the power of magnets in relation to health. The phenomena of magnetism seemed quite miraculous in the early eighteenth century and it was thought possible that it might somehow have an effect upon disease. A number of persons had been working with magnets. One of them was Father Maximilian Hell, court astrologer to the empress of Austria and Mesmer's friend. Father Hell lent Mesmer his magnets for an experiment.

In July of 1774 Mesmer performed his first magnetic "cure." The patient was a young lady who suffered from violent attacks of convulsions, headaches, delirium, and partial paralysis. Mesmer came to this patient when one of her attacks was just beginning, and laid the magnets upon her. She went into furious convulsions, but these subsided almost immediately and she felt better. Normally such attacks lasted for hours. The next day the magnets seemed to have the same salutatory effect upon the patient.

Mesmer asserted that he had cured many other patients with his magnetic treatments, but he could not convince the medical establishment of Vienna that the magnets did any good. Ultimately they made his life so uncomfortable that he was forced to flee Vienna entirely.

In 1778, Mesmer arrived in Paris, a city filled with rich and bored aristocrats hungry for novelty. He set himself up in an elegant mansion on the Place Vendome, and began performing his magnetic cures. Within two years he was a sensation, and his rooms were crowded with the wealthy and powerful, the only ones who could afford his expensive treatments. Even when Mesmer offered his treatments free of charge to the poor, they rarely came forth. They didn't trust this "newfangled" cure.

Mesmer's method of treatment had changed considerably since he had first performed cures by putting magnets upon his patients' bodies. He had abandoned the magnets entirely. The magnetism Mesmer now spoke of was "animal magnetism," a universal force or fluid which controlled health or illness. The doctor, or magnetizer, could direct this force in a number of ways in order to heal his patient. Usually the magnetizer manipulated the force by motions of his hands, or by the traditional "laying on of hands." Mesmer's theories had a plausible scientific sound in the eighteenth century, but in practice, he employed all the traditional regalia and ritual of the sorcerer.

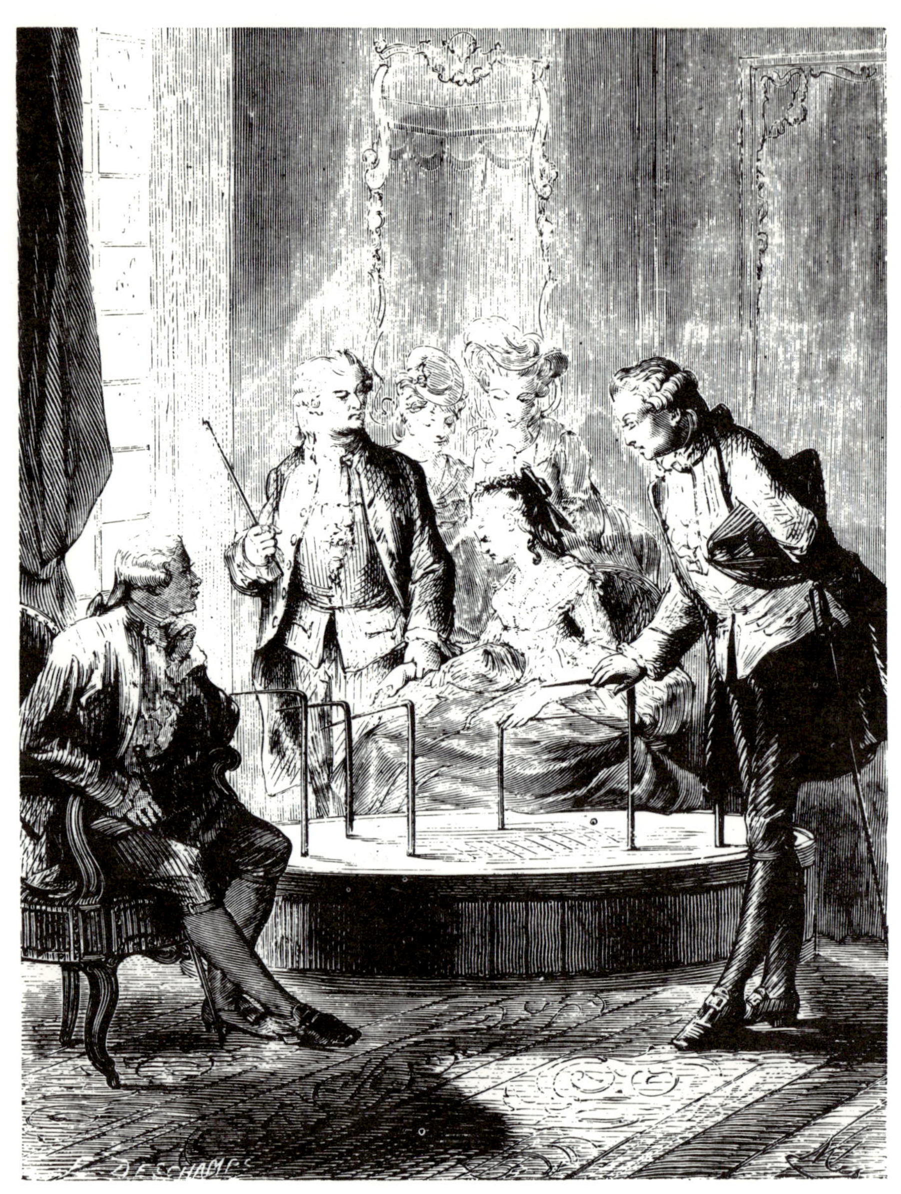

Mesmer's magnetic baquet.

Patients were led into an elegantly appointed room, in the center of which stood Mesmer's *baquet*, a large wooden tub filled with bottles of "magnetic water." From the tub radiated iron rods that were supposed to direct the "magnetic rays."

To get patients into the proper mood, soft music was played. They were then asked to touch hands and form a "magnetic ring." Sometimes they were tied lightly together by a rope. The tension that had built up in anticipation of the "magnetic treatment" was tremendous and quite soon some of the patients began to laugh or cry hysterically. Mesmer's assistants would pass among them, touching those who still held their emotions in check with "magnetic rods."

When the scene had become appropriately frenzied, Mesmer himself would make a dramatic appearance. He wore a lavender robe embroidered with golden flowers, and carried a wand. Walking from patient to patient Mesmer would touch them with his wand and gaze deeply into their eyes. This would send most of the patients into violent convulsions during which they screamed, vomited, and began spitting blood. After a while they would collapse from sheer exhaustion. But when they awoke, they generally felt better.

Mesmer did not invent this healing technique. Any primitive witch doctor or modern faith healer employs pretty much the same methods. They would simply explain their success (or excuse their failures) differently. The witch doctor would say that he was controlling the spirits, the faith healer that he was invoking the spirit of God. Mesmer said he was directing the flow of animal magnetism. No matter what the explanation, these techniques do work in many cases, if the patients have faith in the healer. We know that many ailments are psychosomatic, that there is no physical cause for the illness, though the affliction itself is quite real. A person who believes that he will be cured of such an ailment, can be cured. Even in the case of organically caused ailments, belief is a powerful factor. The person who really believes that he is going to recover, usually recovers faster than a seriously depressed patient.

Aside from dressing like a sorcerer Mesmer used another ancient magical technique—he was very secretive about his treatment. Though he talked quite freely about his theory of animal magnetism, the exact method by which this force was manipulated to cure disease was never revealed.

The king of France was so impressed by Mesmer's cures that he offered the healer a generous pension, if he would set up a school to teach the secrets of the magnetic treatment. Mesmer turned down the offer claiming that to be party to such a bargain would be beneath the dignity of the great truth that he proclaimed. Shortly after he refused the king's pension, Mesmer opened up his own school where, upon payment of an extremely high initiation fee, wealthy gentlemen could learn the secrets of mesmerism.

Mesmer's disciples were called the Society of Harmony and the group functioned more like a traditional secret society than a scientific society. There were regular initiation rites, and the meetings seemed to involve a full Masonic-like ritual filled with symbolism, special passwords, and secret handshakes. In the initiation ceremony the new members recited a religious oath and placed themselves in a mesmeric "rapport" with the director of the ceremony, who embraced them saying, "Go forth, touch, cure."

The Society of Harmony quickly proved to be anything but harmonious. First the members quarreled with Mesmer himself, who was generally considered a pretty quarrelsome character. Then they began bickering with one another, and finally the society broke up entirely, each member going off to practice and preach his own particular brand of mesmerism. Each member also seemed to have acquired a very different understanding of what the true secret of mesmerism was supposed to be.

When he first arrived in Paris, Mesmer eagerly sought to have the scientific and medical establishment give his system a trial but he was rebuffed. The people who flocked to Mesmer cared not one bit for scientific and medical respectability. The physicians couldn't cure them and Mesmer could, that was all that counted. The more patients that Mesmer got, the more impossible it became to ignore his

Mesmer's "animal magnetism" was often pictured as a force that flowed from the hands of the magnetizer.

system. Finally, the king appointed two commissions to study animal magnetism. But by this time Mesmer was no longer inclined to be co-operative. He suspected, probably quite correctly, that the commissions were stacked with his opponents, and his system didn't stand a chance. So he refused to be examined and the commissions were forced to study the work of one of his followers.

The investigation had its comic side. One of the members of the commission was Benjamin Franklin, then serving as American ambassador in France, and a widely respected scientific figure. The mesmerist "magnetized" a tree in the yard of Franklin's house. Then he brought the subject, a twelve-year-old boy, into the yard blindfolded, and led him from tree to tree. In front of one of the trees the boy developed convulsions and collapsed. But it was the wrong tree; he had never gotten within twenty-five feet of the magnetized tree.

Both commissions concluded that they could find no evidence of Mesmer's magnetic fluid. Moreover they said that because of the violent convulsions produced by mesmerism the practice was dangerous and should be suppressed. However, the commissioners were not blind to the fact that something happened during a magnetic session, and that the magnetizer himself had power over his patient.

While the patients still came to Mesmer for treatment, he had been badly stung by the findings of the commissions and decided to leave Paris. Shortly thereafter the French Revolution broke out and no one in France worried about mesmerism for a number of years. Mesmer moved on to Switzerland, where he lived as a country doctor, and later on received a pension from the French government by way of compensation for the property confiscated from him during the Revolution. When Mesmer died in 1815 at the age of eighty-one, he was all but forgotten. The doctrine of mesmerism, however, was very much alive.

For all his showmanship and crankiness, Franz Mesmer was quite sincere in his belief that he had discovered a revolutionary principle of healing. He attributed the effects that he produced in his patients to the universal fluid called animal magnetism. More recently scientists have abandoned the idea of animal magnetism and attribute the effects of mesmerism, or hypnotism as it is now called, to the power of suggestion. There is a great deal that we still do not know about hypnotism, but it can no longer be classed as an occult or magical practice. For well over a century, however, mesmerism figured heavily in occult theories. No would-be wonder-worker of the nineteenth or early twentieth century failed to attribute at least some of his effects to mesmerism or magnetism.

Mesmer's pupil, the Marquis de Puységur, changed Mesmer's system somewhat. Instead of sending his subjects into violent convulsions, which he found upsetting to observe, he simply put them to sleep. It was Puységur who coined the term somnambulist, or artificial sleepwalker. His most successful somnambulist was a peasant named Victor, who was not only cured of his lung disease, but while in a magnetic trance seemed able to read minds and diagnose diseases.

Victor was only the first in a long line of somnambulists who seemed to possess extraordinary powers while entranced. This was not a new development. Since ancient times, prophets and other magical types had often gone into trances before working their wonders. Mesmerism merely gave these ancient practices an up-to-date and more acceptable terminology.

Eliphas Levi, the nineteenth-century occultist and highly unorthodox Catholic, discussed mesmerism and somnambulism as part of magic:

> The Church in its great wisdom forbids us to consult oracles and to violate by indiscreet curiosity the secrets of futurity. In our day the voice of the Church is no longer heeded; the people go back to diviners and phythonesses; the somnambulists have become the prophets for those who believe no longer in Gospel precepts.

Somnambulists were also believed to be in contact with the world of the spirits. The whole extraordinary phenomenon known as modern spiritualism was heavily influenced by the theories and the followers of Mesmer.

For a time the magnetist or mesmerist was regarded as the most powerful form of magician. The evil mesmerist Svengali in the novel *Trilby* was as much a sorcerer as anything else. The theory grew that the mesmerist possessed some sort of special power which gave him absolute control over other people. Mary Baker Eddy, founder of Christian Science, believed that malicious animal magnetism, controlled and directed by evil mesmerists, was responsible for much of the world's suffering. Later Christian Scientists pretty well abandoned this belief.

Like Paracelsus, Mesmer made a contribution both to the world of science and to the world of magic. He was perhaps the last person in history to be able to straddle both worlds.

7
THE NEW WORLD OF MAGIC

THE NINETEENTH AND EARLY TWENTIETH CENTURIES

THE MAGICIAN of today often looks and acts like the sorcerer of old. He may wear robes or other bizarre dress. He can draw magic diagrams, chant spells, burn incense, and dispense charms and amulets —but there is a fundamental difference. Few magicians of the last century or two have claimed to be able to produce real physical changes in the world. According to one recent definition, magic is "the science and art of creating changes in consciousness."

The principal force in modern magic is believed to be the human will. All the elements of ceremonial magic, the rituals, the chants, the diagrams, the incense, are simply means of concentrating the will of the magician. However, the difference between the mental magic of modern times and the physical magic of past ages is not always clear, even to the magician. Modern magicians have rarely tried to make gold from lead by the operation of pure will (though this has been attempted), but they have often tried to cause physical harm to their enemies by an act of will.

Another fundamental belief of modern magic is that there are non-physical planes of existence, inhabited by various sorts of nonhuman or superhuman intelligences. These intelligences have been given a variety of names: the adepts, the illuminated ones, the masters, the mahatmas, the secret chiefs, the Great White Lodge, even the space intelligences. Only the greatest or boldest of the modern magicians have claimed to be in direct contact with these beings. Much of modern magic is concerned with various studies and tests that are aimed at "purifying" the novice, so that he can communicate with the masters.

Still another principle is that the ancients possessed powers that modern man, with all his technology, has lost. But the knowledge has not entirely disappeared; it is still contained in ancient documents, rituals, and ceremonies. These seem mysterious, obscure, and to the uninitiated, utterly incomprehensible and even foolish, but for those who hold the key, the power is there. For the modern student of magic the desire to penetrate these mysteries becomes an obsession, as strong as that which gripped the medieval alchemist. The would-be magician of today is as immune to disappointment as were his predecessors. When one magical teacher fails to provide the answers, he goes to another and another, always feeling sure that the next magical master will be the one to lift the veil and reveal to him the secrets of the ages. The world of students of magic has been splendidly described by one of the most colorful figures of modern magic, Madame Helena Petrovena Blavatsky, in her *Secret Doctrine*:

Alone a handful of primitive men—in whom the spark of Divine Wisdom burnt bright, and only strengthened in its intensity as it got dimmer and dimmer with every age in those who turned it to bad purposes—remained the elect custodians of the Mysteries revealed to mankind by the Divine Teachers. There were among them those who remained in their Kumaric condition (divine purity) from the beginning; and tradition whispers, that the secret teachings affirm, that these elect were the germ of a Hierarchy; which never died since that period.

ELIPHAS LEVI AND THE FRENCH MAGICIANS

According to all the magical texts the magician's creed is "to know, to dare, to will, and to keep silent." Eliphas Levi claimed to know, dare, and will, but he was never able to keep silent. He became the most prolific and influential writer on magic since the time of Agrippa.

Eliphas Levi, or Alphonse Louis Constant, to give his real name, was born in Paris in the year 1810. His father was a shoemaker and poor, as shoemakers generally were. But the boy was bright and showed considerable interest in religion. Through the good offices of a parish priest, he was enrolled in St. Sulpice, and he seemed destined for a church career. Though he progressed a fair way into his studies, young Constant was always rebellious. Ultimately he was expelled for holding "strange doctrines," though no one seems sure of what these doctrines were.

After his expulsion from St. Sulpice, Levi became a follower of a weird individual called Ganneau who preached revolution in order to restore the French monarchy. Ganneau believed that he was the reincarnation of Louis XVI and his wife of Marie Antoinette. Levi was actually imprisoned briefly for his activities on behalf of the sect. Finally he became disillusioned with this royalist messiah. For a time Levi supported himself as a writer, usually of extremely conservative Catholic propaganda. That was one odd thing about Eliphas Levi—though he held wildly unorthodox views about magic and religion, and had been expelled from a seminary, he remained at heart a thoroughly conservative Catholic. Indeed, his views on the Church were more those of the fifteenth century, than of the nineteenth century. Perhaps it was this romantic longing for the past that led Levi to the study of what he believed to be the ancient doctrines of magic. Throughout his career he tried to reconcile his magical ideas with his Catholic beliefs, but the attempt was always clumsy and unsuccessful. Levi's appeal then as now, is to occultists outside of formal religion rather than to orthodox Catholics.

While studying for the priesthood Levi had taken a vow of celibacy and he never officially renounced this vow. But when he was in his thirties, he married a beautiful and spirited girl of sixteen. The marriage was a short and disastrous one, and was quickly annulled. It was only after the breakup of his marriage that Eliphas Levi plunged deeply into the study of the occult sciences. For over a decade Levi was immersed in his strange studies and little is known of his whereabouts.

Then early in the 1850's Levi published his magnum opus *The Dogma and Ritual of High Magic*. This was followed by *History of Magic*, *Key to the Great Mysteries*, and a few other volumes. Levi contended that magic was a secret tradition handed down in veiled and obscure symbols from the ancient Magi. For the content of this magical tradition Levi drew upon alchemy, the cabala, tarot cards, Rosicrucianism, Freemasonry, mesmerism, and the works of other occultists like the Englishman Francis Barrett. There is little that is original in his work, and even his admirers warn that neither his interpretations nor his facts are to be trusted. An English translation of Levi's *History of Magic* by the occult scholar A. E. Wate is loaded with footnotes correcting Levi's errors.

Yet despite these shortcomings, or perhaps because of them, Levi has had an impact. His writing style was best described as nineteenth-century Gothic. Even his description of what was originally a simple ritual of drawing a protective magic circle on the ground had an awesome and mysterious tone to it:

> In a sinister place, by the light of a fire kindled with broken crucifixes, a circle is traced with the embers of a burnt crucifix reciting while doing so a magical hymn containing verses from the psalms of David.

Levi didn't make much money from his books while he was alive. They are probably more popular now than they were when first published. His life displays one of the great paradoxes of the magician; though he claimed to possess great power, it seemed to do him no

Eliphas Levi.

worldly good. He scraped out a living by offering lessons to aspiring occultists. Judging from the wreck of his marriage his personal life could not have been a very happy one. He would doubtless argue that the rewards of magic need not be material, though material rewards are certainly among the promises made by the magician. But even if the rewards of magic were purely spiritual, they were not sufficient for Eliphas Levi; by the end of his life he had become completely reconciled with Catholicism. When he died in 1875, it was the last rites of the Roman Catholic church, rather than any magical ritual that comforted him.

An English occultist who visited Levi in Paris described him this way:

> I found him a short burly man, with a rubicund complexion, very small but piercing eyes, twinkling with good humor, his face broad, his lips small and well compressed together, nostrils dilating. The lower part of his face was covered with a thick black beard and moustache, and I noticed that his ears were small and delicate. In person he was lusty, and his dress was plain and quiet. Upon his head he wore a kind of felt hat turned up in front. On removing his hat to salute me, I observed that his head was partially bald, his hair dark and glistening, and that portion of his skull, which had been submitted to the tonsure, was partially overgrown with hair.
>
> He apologized for wearing his hat, stating that he was compelled to do so by an affliction of his head, which rendered it dangerous for him to remain uncovered.

Levi showed his English visitor some of his extensive collection of magical manuscripts, implements, and drawings, but he performed no ceremonies, and conjured no demons. In general, Levi seems to have preferred theorizing about magic than actually trying to perform it. He is known to have attempted only one magical operation, raising the ghost of the ancient magician Apollonius of Tyana. This happened in 1854 when Levi visited London, and a description of this little act of necromancy should give you an idea of the sort of magic Eliphas Levi advocated.

He prepared himself by fasting for twenty-one days. Numerology gets in here for three and seven are powerful magic numbers and three times seven is twenty-one. Levi was alone when the ceremony was performed, thus we have only his word for what happened. The magical paraphernalia was comparatively simple. The ceremonial room had four concave mirrors and an altar covered with a new white lambskin. A pentagram (five-pointed star) was carved on top of the altar. There were two chafing dishes, one on the altar, the other on a tripod. Levi wore a white robe. All this white was supposed to indicate that he was practicing white as opposed to black magic. On the magician's head was a wreath of vervain leaves, useful in warding off demons. In one hand he held a sword, in the other a copy of the ritual.

Fires were lit in the chafing dishes, and Levi began a long incantation: "In unity the demons chant the praises of God; they lose their malice and fury . . . Cerberus opens his triple jaw, and fire chants the praises of God with the three tongues of the lightning. . . . the soul revisits the tombs, the magical lamps are lighted . . ." As the chant rose in pitch Levi felt the ground shake, and he thought he saw a figure of a man standing before the altar, but the figure vanished.

The magician repeated the incantation and this time something seemed to stir in the depths of the mirrors. Levi closed his eyes and summoned three times for the ghost to appear. "When I again looked forth there was a man in front of me, wrapped from head to foot in a species of shroud, which seemed more gray than white; he was lean, melancholy and beardless."

Levi now felt abnormally cold, and badly frightened. He tried to command the spirit but was unable to speak properly. Something touched his sword arm, which went numb to the elbow. He was overcome by intense weakness and fainted.

For several days after the ceremony, Levi's arm was sore. The two questions he had intended to ask the ghost had never been asked, but Levi felt they had been answered in his mind. The answers were "death" and "dead." He did not reveal the questions.

When it came to explaining what had happened, Eliphas Levi was obscure and even contradictory. He did not believe he had really seen the ghost of Apollonius, but rather that the intense strain of the ceremony had produced, "an actual drunkenness of the imagination." Yet he said that he had seen and touched something real. "I do not explain the physical laws by which I saw and touched; I affirm solely

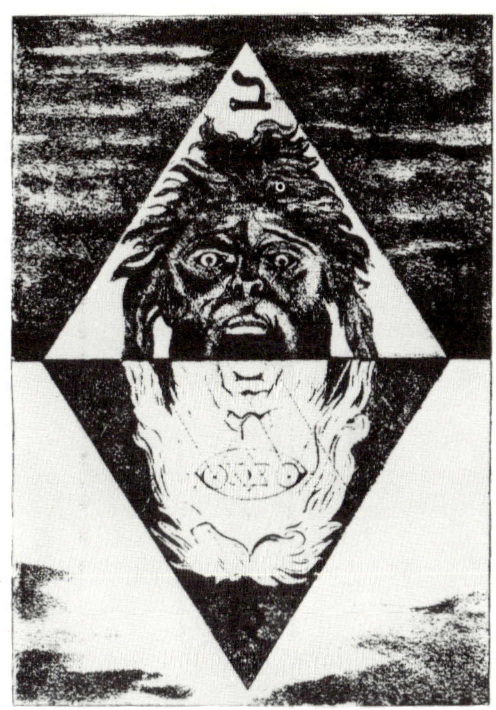

Cabalistic diagrams used in the books of Eliphas Levi.

that I did see and that I did touch, that I saw clearly and distinctly, apart from dreaming, and this is sufficient to establish the real efficacy of magical ceremonies . . . I command the greatest caution to those who propose devoting themselves to similar experiences; their result is intense exhaustion, and frequently a shock sufficient to occasion illness."

While Levi was practicing his rather gentle magic, another group of French sorcerers were engaging in a furious battle of bewitchment. On one side was a defrocked priest called Abbé Boullan, who led a sect called the Work of Mercy. Despite the rather bland title, the group seems to have been engaged primarily in sex orgies with black magic rituals.

In 1886 the Boullan group was visited by a young occultist, Marquis Stanislas de Guaita. Guaita was disgusted by what he saw, and the following year joined forces with one of Boullan's former followers, Oswald Wirth. The two announced that they had judged Boullan and condemned him. Later they said that they merely meant to expose him as a scoundrel, but Boullan believed that the pair was out to destroy him by black magic.

Though it is tempting to regard Boullan as a cynical faker, there is no doubt that his terror in the face of a magical attack was quite genuine. Boullan was assisted by a clairvoyant who said she saw Boullan's enemies putting his portrait in a coffin—trying to kill him by imitative magic. Next she saw them saying a black mass against him. The black mass is an obscene parody of the Catholic Mass, and is used for summoning demons. Boullan retaliated with a series of frantic anathemas, conjurations, and incantations, but these seemed to have no effect upon his foe. The novelist J. B. Huysmans, a friend of Boullan's, wrote, "Boullan jumps about like a tiger cat, clutching one of his hosts (communion wafers marked with blood and commonly used by black magicians) and invoking the aid of St. Michael and the eternal justicares of eternal justice. Then standing at his altar he cries, 'Strike down Peldan,' (one of the Guaita group) . . ."

The climax of this bizarre magical warfare was reached in 1893.

On January 3, Boullan wrote to Huysmans, saying that the new year was one of ill omen. "The figures 8-9-3 form a combination which foreshadows bad news. [Boullan did not explain this but a possible explanation is that 8 + 9 + 3 = 20 and 2 + 0 = 2, the number of the Devil. This sort of calculation was and is still common in numerology.] During the previous night Julie Thibault [the clairvoyant] dreamed of Guaita and in the early hours of the morning a black bird of death cried out. It was the herald of the attack." By the next day, January 4, Abbé Boullan was dead.

Boullan's friends were convinced that he had been killed by Guaita's sorcery and said so in print. As a result a real duel, with pistols, was arranged between Guaita and Jules Bois, one of Boullan's supporters. Each side did its best to disconcert the other by magic. On his way to the duel one of Bois' carriage horses had a fit, and Bois was convinced magic was responsible. In the duel itself each man fired once but no one was hit. Three days later Bois fought another duel with a member of the Guaita group. This time his carriage overturned on the way to the duel. He arrived battered and bleeding, but in the duel, that was fought with swords, no one was hurt. The ending of the famed magical battle was almost comic.

MAC GREGOR MATHERS AND THE GOLDEN DAWN

The Golden Dawn, one of the most influential magical societies in the modern English-speaking world, had a romantic beginning. The idea for it originated with one of those mysterious documents, which seem to turn up so regularly in the history of magic. In 1884, according to one account, a clergyman named Dr. Woodman found a strange coded manuscript in an obscure London bookstall. In another version the coded manuscript was found by Dr. Woodman among the papers of a mystic and reputed magician named Fred Hockley who died in 1855.

Dr. Woodman had long been interested in occultism, but the manuscript was meaningless to him. He took it to his friend Dr. William Wynn Wescott, a physician, occult scholar, and a leading member of the *Societas Rosicruciana in Anglia*, an English Rosicrucian group. Dr. Wescott made some sort of a translation, but he was unsure and desired a second opinion. He called in S. L. Mathers, a young museum curator who had a good reputation as a scholar of the occult. Mathers was enthusiastic. The manuscripts seemed to contain rituals and formulas by which students could obtain magical powers, and ultimately contact the hidden adepts.

Dr. Wescott, Mathers, and a few like-minded friends formed a society called the Hermetic Order of the Golden Dawn. The structure of the Order was similar to that of magical secret societies of the past. The neophyte passed through the grades of Zelator, Theoricus, Practicus, and Philosophus to the Portal grade, which prepared him for the "Reception of Light"; beyond this was the grade of Adeptus Minor, which was supposed to connect the candidate with his "Higher Genius." The ritual of initiation took place in a seven-sided chamber modeled after the tomb of Christian Rosenkreuz.

Initiation as Adeptus Minor completed the training in the First Order, or Outer Order. The candidate then advanced to the Second Order, or Inner Order, which also had a series of initiation ceremonies and titles. Then there was the Third Order or "the Secret Chiefs." These beings were invisible, immortal, omnipotent, and virtually unreachable, except by the most advanced and talented occultists. Few were bold enough to claim that they had contact with "the Secret Chiefs."

At every level of advancement the members of the Golden Dawn swore oaths of absolute secrecy. But the members proved to be so eccentric and touchy that they could keep nothing secret for very long.

Esoteric occultism was popular in England in the 1880's and the Golden Dawn prospered in a small way. At first there was only the Isis-Urania Temple in London, but soon it was joined by an Osiris Temple in Weston-super-Mare, a Horus Temple in Bradford, an Amen-Ra Temple in Edinburgh, and ultimately an Ahathoor Temple in Paris for Englishmen living on the continent. The temples were given the names of ancient Egyptian gods and goddesses.

At its height in the 1890's, the Golden Dawn never had more than one hundred active members, but some were extremely prominent. An early member was the Irish poet and Nobel Prize winner, William Butler Yeats. Yeats introduced the actress Florence Farr to the Dawn. Two writers of excellent supernatural fiction, Algernon Blackwood and Arthur Machen, also joined up. Aleister Crowley, one of the evilest black magicians, got his start with the Golden Dawn, too.

In the early days it was Wescott and Mathers who dominated the group. Then in 1897 Wescott resigned. It was rumored that he was told to resign from the Golden Dawn or lose his profitable government position as coroner of London. More likely he finally just got fed up with Mathers, who was a difficult man at best, and decided to devote his energies to the more respectable *Societas Rosicruciana in Anglia*, where he had risen to the position of Supreme Magus (supreme magician).

Of all the Dawn members, Mathers was one of the most flamboyant and the most important. S. L. Mathers was born in 1854, the son of a London clerk. He became interested in occultism while young and soon developed a reputation as an occult scholar, and translator of odd and rare books.

Mathers married a French woman, and in 1894 moved to Paris, but he still managed to control the affairs of the Golden Dawn across the Channel.

Aside from his interest in Hermetic magic, Mathers also became fascinated by Celtic romanticism, and while in Paris he generally went about in full Highland Scots dress, kilts and all. He was clearly dissatisfied with his own humble origins, and began calling himself, MacGregor Mathers, and the Count MacGregor of Glenstrae. These bogus names and titles distressed some of the more staid members of the Golden Dawn, and created a good deal of general confusion. Once, while testifying at a trial, the court had some difficulty in establishing who Mathers really was:

Is it a fact that your name is Samuel Liddel Mathers?

—Yes, or MacGregor Mathers.

Your original name was Samuel Liddell Mathers?

—Undoubtedly.

Did you subsequently assume the name of MacGregor?

—The name of MacGregor dates from 1603.

Your name was MacGregor in 1603?

—Yes, if you like to put it that way.

You have called yourself Count MacGregor of Glenstrae?

—Oh, yes!

You have called yourself the Chevalier MacGregor?

—No, you are confusing me with one of Crowley's aliases.

Have you ever suggested to anyone that you had any connection with King James IV of Scotland?

—I do not quite understand your question. Every Scotsman of ancient family must have some connection with King James IV.

Have you ever stated that King James IV of Scotland never died?

—Yes, that is a matter of common tradition among occult bodies . . .

Do you assert that King James IV is in existence today?

—I refuse to answer your question.

And that his existence today is embodied in yourself?

—Certainly not!

Do you claim that Cagliostro never died and that you are him?

—Certainly not, you are again confusing me with one of Crowley's aliases.

Mathers and his wife Moina lived in a house decorated to look like an Egyptian temple. When not wearing his Highland garb, Mathers could be seen in a long white robe, a metal belt engraved with the signs of the zodiac, bracelets round his wrists and ankles, and a leopard skin slung across his shoulders. Along with his Scottish names, Mathers like all other members of the Golden Dawn adopted magical names. His were S' Rhioghail Mo Dhream (Royal is my Race) and Deo Duce Comite Ferro (With God as My Leader and the Sword as my Companion). Generally his fellow magical initiates referred to him by his initials S.R.M.D. or D.D.C.F.

The Mathers' household may well have been the oddest in all Paris. Yeats, who was a frequent visitor, recalled playing four-handed chess. Yeats and Mrs. Mathers opposed Mathers and a ghost. Mathers moved the ghost's pieces, but before doing so he would shade his eyes and stare earnestly at the empty chair on the other side of the board.

Mathers claimed that he, and he alone, was in contact with the invisible Secret Chiefs. They regularly appeared to him at midnight in the Bois de Boulogne in Paris. His pronouncements, therefore, bore the stamp of absolute authority. Over the years Mathers became increasingly autocratic, and the other members of the order increasingly restless.

The final straw came in 1900 when Mathers initiated Aleister Crowley as an Adeptus Minor of the Order, a high position for a new member. Crowley was still young and just starting his sensational career as an occultist, but he had already acquired a well-deserved bad reputation. For all their eccentricity most of the members of the Golden Dawn were respectable Englishmen and women who wanted nothing to do with a man like Crowley who really enjoyed shocking the public. The London branch of the Dawn specifically refused Crowley's initiation, so Crowley went to Paris where Mathers showed complete disregard of everyone else's opinion and initiated Crowley himself.

Mathers then sent Crowley to London with orders to take over the Isis-Urania Temple, and throw out everyone who opposed him (Mathers). The rebels in London tried to thwart Crowley by an occult attack. Crowley said that as a result of the attack against him his rubber mackintosh burst into flames, he became obsessed and bad-tempered, and horses ran away from him.

Crowley responded by magically evoking an evil spirit against the man he thought to be leader of the revolt. When this failed he tried more direct action. He hired a gang of bully boys from a local pub and physically took over the London temple. The rebels responded by calling the police, and notifying Crowley's creditors that he was in town. With that Aleister Crowley had had enough and retired from the fight.

Meanwhile back in Paris, MacGregor Mathers was not inactive. He took a packet of dried peas and baptized each one with the magical name of one of the rebels. Then, by the formula of the Great Enochian Tablet of Spirit, he evoked the forces of Beelzebub and Typhon-Set and, while shaking the peas in a sieve called upon these mighty devils to fall upon his enemies and confound them with quarrels and disruptions. Perhaps the spell worked, for the rebels soon fell to fighting among themsleves. The revolt was broken but that didn't help Mathers much. He tried to reassert his control, but by that time the Golden Dawn was hopelessly split. All Mathers got was one of the numerous splinter groups, each one of which claimed to be a legitimate descendant of the true Golden Dawn.

It was inevitable that Mathers and his once fanatically loyal disciple, Crowley, would have a falling out. Two such gigantic egos could not coexist for long. By 1904 they were hurtling magical thunderbolts at one another. Mathers sent a "vampire" to destroy Crowley, but according to Crowley he "smote her (the vampire) with her own current of evil." Crowley claimed that Mathers' black magic had killed his pet bloodhounds, and in response he evoked Beelzebub against Mathers. Both combatants survived the magical duel unscathed.

Despite all his claims to magical power, occult knowledge, and an aristocratic family, life was not kind to S. L. Mathers. In the early years of the Golden Dawn he had essentially been supported by a wealthy occultist, Miss A. E. F. Horniman. But they had a bitter quarrel, and Mathers lost his allowance. From then on he supported himself by selling Turkish Railway shares on commission, and occasional handouts from other occultists. It was an erratic living, and for many of his Paris years, Mathers lived in wretched poverty. He died of influenza in 1918.

Mathers' magic had never made him rich and powerful as he might have desired. But Mathers believed, and many occultists agreed, that the Golden Dawn under his direction was genuinely attempting to probe ancient magical knowledge. Mathers' defenders acknowledge that he was something of a showman, perhaps even a bit of a madman, but he knew a great deal about the ancient traditions of magic. His tragedy, say the occultists, was that he didn't know quite enough to make the magic work properly. Modern students of magic say that in its early days, the Golden Dawn was operating in the genuine magical tradition. Later, as personality conflicts developed between the members and as Mathers himself became more and more autocratic, the purity of the group declined.

After Mathers' death his widow, Moina, tried to take over the leadership of the Golden Dawn, but the now shaky society sank even lower under her erratic guidance. Before the First World War it had been rumored that Mathers initiated some wealthy Americans into the society, and that one could rise to any grade, not by occult study, but by payment of a high fee. Mrs. Mathers went further by commissioning an occult correspondence course in America.

The rest of Moina Mathers' career is unimportant, except for one rather grim incident. All the occult attacks and cursing that went on among the feuding members of the Golden Dawn seems exotically amusing and harmless enough. In the great majority of cases it was, but the results could, on occasion, be deadly. Moina Mathers was a great one for launching magical attacks against her enemies. One of them, a rising young occultist who called herself Dion Fortune, claimed that she had been "desperately afflicted with black cats" by Mrs. Mathers, and that one morning "I suddenly saw coming down the stairs towards me, a gigantic tabby cat, twice the size of a tiger." Dion Fortune exorcised the cats and other evil influences. Miss Netta Fornario, a minor member of one of the Golden Dawn offshoots, could not exorcise her demons so successfully.

In the autumn of 1929 Miss Fornario traveled to the island of Iona, off the western coast of Scotland. The purpose of her visit was unknown, though she indicated that she had occult reasons. After two months on the island she awoke one morning in a state of panic. She told her landlady, in a somewhat disjointed fashion, that she had to leave immediately because "certain people" were affecting her telepathically. But no boat was available for several days. Later in the day she emerged from her room with what her landlady described as "a calm look of resignation of her face," and said that she had decided to stay on Iona indefinitely.

The next morning she was missing. Searchers found her body near the ruins of an ancient village. She was wearing a black cloak, of the kind used in Golden Dawn ceremonies, and she had a silver chain around her neck. Otherwise she was naked. In her hand was a large steel knife which had been used to cut a cross in the turf. The soles of her feet were badly torn, indicating that she had run a considerable distance. The examining physician said she had died of heart failure.

The mysterious death stirred up a furor in London occult circles. Dion Fortune said that without a doubt Miss Fornario had been killed by magic, and that the magician was Moina Mathers. As evidence she said that Miss Fornario's body had been scratched and that the victims of Mrs. Mathers' "astral attacks" always bore the marks of scratches.

Certainly the death was not caused by magic. But as we have seen the belief in magic can itself be a powerful force. In primitive societies an individual who knows that he has been cursed may actually sicken and die. The same thing can happen in civilized societies, where there are individuals who believe deeply enough in magic.

ALEISTER CROWLEY

Some people said that Aleister Crowley was possessed by a demon, and that they knew the exact moment at which this possession took place. In 1909, Crowley and his friend Victor Neuburg were in Algiers. They decided to go out into the desert to summon up a "mighty devil" called Choronzon.

The first part of the summoning was to draw a magic circle in the sand. So long as the circle remained unbroken, the demon was not supposed to be able to get inside of it, and so the magicians would be protected. Some other magical figures were drawn in the sand and the name of Choronzon was written three times in the form of a triangle. The two magicians cut the throats of three pigeons, one at each angle of the triangle, and poured the blood onto the sand. The blood was supposed to give the demon power to become visible.

Crowley himself sat in the triangle, rather than in the protective circle, wearing a black robe and hood that covered his head except for eye slits. Crowley was going to allow the demon to take possession of him for the ceremony.

He took a topaz and, staring into it, saw the image of the demon in its depths. Then he cried out the words which are supposed to open the gates of Hell, *Zazas, Zazas, Nasatanada, Zazas.* The demon then took possession of Crowley's body.

Neuburg saw neither Crowley nor the demon but a beautiful woman, who spoke enticingly to him. He then realized that it was the Choronzon trying to fool him and get into the circle. The woman then disappeared, and was replaced by the demon himself. He promised to serve Neuburg if only he could come inside the circle and put his head at Neuburg's feet. This was recognized as another trick. The demon then appeared as Crowley, begging for water to quench his thirst. Still Neuburg refused to break the circle and tried to command the demon to obey him. But the demon was not to be ordered about, and he appeared in his own form again and threatened Neuburg with all the torments of hell.

Neuburg attempted to write down what the demon was saying, and while he was thus distracted Choronzon threw some sand on the line of the magic circle. With the circle broken the demon rushed into it and tried to tear Neuburg's throat out with his fangs. Neuburg protected himself by invoking the Names of God and stabbing the demon with a magic knife. Finally the demon was forced back and Neuburg repaired the circle.

After a couple more tries at deception the demon admitted defeat, but by this time the energy contained in the pigeon blood had been exhausted, and the ceremony came to an end.

Crowley said that he had observed the entire ceremony, and that the demon had no form, but was "the terror of darkness, and the blindness of night, and the deafness of the adder, and the tastelessness of stale and stagnant water, and the black fire of hatred, and the udders of the Cat of slime; not one thing but many things."

Some say that Crowley simply invented this whole incident, others that it was the result of a hallucination. But there are those who claim that Aleister Crowley really did summon up a demon, and that the demon never left him.

There is certainly something demonic about Crowley's career, but the evil began before 1909.

Aleister Crowley was born in 1875 into a family that belonged to the Plymouth Brethren, a highly puritanical and austere British Protestant sect. He spent the rest of his life frantically doing the opposite of everything his parents had taught him.

Crowley had two great advantages, an inheritance of some £14,000 and a magnificent physique. He ran through his inheritance rather quickly, but his health remained excellent for years despite ingesting quantities of drink and drugs that would have killed half a dozen ordinary men.

Occultism had attracted Crowley when he was quite young, and while a student at Cambridge he began writing strange mystic erotic poetry which he published (at his own expense) in elegant little volumes.

In London, Crowley lived under the name "Count Svaroff." He bought an estate in Scotland, called himself "Laird of Boleskine," and took to wearing kilts. He then met another kilt-wearing occultist, MacGregor Mathers, and was initiated into the Golden Dawn under the secret name Frater Perdurabo. Eventually, Crowley had problems with the Golden Dawn, in a battle of magical egos, and after the confrontation he took off for the Far East where he did some spectacular mountain climbing. There was a rumor that during one of the expeditions, food ran short and Crowley ate two of his porters. While in the Orient he converted at least briefly to Buddhism. He later tried to

Aleister Crowley.

get his mentor Mathers to convert, but the Supreme Magus of the Golden Dawn would have none of it, and the break between the two widened.

In 1904, Crowley claimed that he was in communication with a nonhuman entity called Aiwass. On the basis of these communications he announced that he was going to set up a new religion to replace Christianity, and start a new Rosicrucian Order with himself as chief. The initiation Crowley proposed for his new order involved such things as affixing the candidate to a cross "in a position to cause some pain," and whipping him repeatedly. This organization did not prove popular, and eventually the plans were abandoned. Crowley then formed the *Astrum Argentinum* or Silver Star. The rituals were stolen from the Golden Dawn with a little bit of Yoga thrown in.

Meanwhile Crowley was involved in constant warfare with his occult enemies and these included practically all of his former friends. In his magazine *The Equinox*, Crowley began publishing the "secret rituals" of other societies. This so alarmed Mathers that he tried to get an injunction to stop publication of *The Equinox* but he was too poor to carry through with the case.

Aleister Crowley was getting into stride now. He had become notorious not only among occultists, but to the public at large. In London he staged a public performance of what he called the Rites of Eleusis. A critic for a publication called the *Looking Glass* described how he was admitted to a darkened room by "a rather dirty looking person attired in a sort of imitation Eastern robe," with a drawn sword in his hand.

A number of hooded persons finally appeared on a stage including Crowley, who was wearing a red hood and who "commenced to read some gibberish to which the attendants made response at intervals." The gibberish was Crowley's poetry. A woman called the Mother of Heaven appeared and played "not unskillfully" on the violin for about ten minutes. The Mother of Heaven was Leila Waddell, the second of Crowley's three wives. Finally some of the figures on the stage asked Crowley, "the Master, is there really a God, as, if not, they will amuse themselves without any fear of the consequences." Crowley retired behind the curtain to give the matter some thought. When he finally emerged he announced that there is no God, and his followers might do whatever they liked.

The *Looking Glass* followed up the review with a series of exposés of Crowley's scandalous private life. The publicity scared away many of the more respectable members of Crowley's order, and the A. A. in England virtually disappeared.

Something else had disappeared at about the same time—Crowley's inheritance. He now had to depend upon magic not merely for notoriety but for a living. Crowley joined up with an organization called the *Ordo Templi Orientis*, or O.T.O. This magical group, founded in Germany by Karl Kellner, was touted as being a descendant of the medieval Knights Templar, a society of fighting monks that had been suppressed by the Church in the fifteenth century for heresy, sodomy, and bestiality. Sex occasionally played a part in the rites of modern magic, but usually it was discussed in such veiled language that the outsider had no idea what the occultist was talking about. Kellner, on the other hand, was quite frank:

"Our Order possesses the KEY which opens up all Masonic and Hermetic secrets, namely, the teaching of sexual magic, and this teaching explains, without exception, all the secrets of Nature, all the symbolism of Freemasonry and all systems of religion."

This was Aleister Crowley's sort of group. He was initiated into the O.T.O. with the title of "Supreme and Holy King of Ireland, Iona and with all the Britains within the Sanctuary of the Gnosis (knowledge)."

Crowley's experiments with "sex magic," and his increasing pro-German sympathies, made London a difficult place for him, and so he departed for America when World War I broke out. In America the Master of Thereon or the "Great Beast," as Crowley liked to call himself, earned money by writing pro-German propaganda and setting up branches of the A.A. and the O.T.O.

One of Crowley's more spectacular feats in America came when he claimed to have spent forty days fasting and meditating on an island in the Hudson River, and wound up by defacing the cliffs south of Kingston, New York, by painting in huge red letters his mottoes:

EVERY MAN AND EVERY WOMAN A STAR!
DO WHAT THOU WILT SHALL BE THE WHOLE OF THE LAW.

In 1919, Crowley moved his activities to the town of Cefalù in Sicily. He bought an old building reputed to have once been a monastery, gathered some of his American and English disciples, and founded what he called the Sacred Abbey of Thelema or the College of the Holy Ghost. Sensational stories of abominable rites and orgies at Cefalù began reaching the British press. There seems to have been a good deal of sex, heavy drug-taking, and some rituals in which Crowley, now quite stout, did a lot of prancing around in the nude waving a sword and chanting his own poetry.

The climax of the Sicilian adventure came when one of Crowley's young followers, Raoul Loveday, died after a rite in which a cat was sacrificed and its blood drunk. Loveday's death seems to have had nothing to do with the ritual itself but resulted from drinking contaminated water. Loveday's enterprising widow sold her firsthand account of Crowley's Sicilian wonderland to the British papers. It was the sacrifice of the cat that really finished Crowley in the eyes of the animal-loving British public.

Despite Crowley's profascist sympathies, Mussolini's government expelled him from Cefalù. Mussolini, who was also trying to rid Sicily of the Mafia and pose as the protector of Christian morality, was doubtless glad to be rid of the notorious pest.

Crowley went to Paris where the police exiled him as a drug peddler. Back in London in 1937 he stood at the foot of the Egyptian obelisk called Cleopatra's Needle and proclaimed that there would be a great war within nine months. Only if everybody followed Aleister Crowley could the catastrophe be averted.

The Great Beast spent the last years of his life wandering forlornly around from England to Germany to Portugal and back again. He had become the undisputed leader of the German-based O.T.O., but when some of his works were translated into German most of the members were so horrified that they resigned. Crowley was too much even for this sex-oriented group. Hitler finally closed down the O.T.O. and all other occult organizations in 1937.

Crowley himself died in England in 1947, worn out by a lifetime of attempting to impress an increasingly indifferent world. The antics of Aleister Crowley, the self-proclaimed "Great Beast," seemed almost funny when compared with the real bestiality of the Nazis.

After World War II an American disciple of Crowley tried reviving Crowley's O.T.O. in California. There were the usual nude rites, but the cult never really got off the ground. The O.T.O. has been re-established in Germany but it is small, and little of Crowley's influence remains.

In the 1970's, a sort of Aleister Crowley revival has been going on. A number of small cults claim to be based on his teachings. Many of his long, obscure, and exceedingly boring books have been reissued and he has become a hero of sorts to the current crop of occultists who like to think of themselves as witches or Satanists. Crowley's fascist leanings and cruel misuse of anyone who was close to him have been forgotten, and he is viewed as the archetype of the anti-establishment figure.

MADAME BLAVATSKY

Of all the exotic and bizarre characters that have peopled the world of magic none was more exotic or bizarre than the Russian adventuress, Madame Helena Petrovena Blavatsky, H.P.B.—or the Old Lady, as she often called herself.

The Old Lady would object violently to being placed in the world of magic. One can almost imagine her shaking with rage and shouting hysterically, "Magic, Magic! What have I to do with magic. I'm no parlor conjurer or carnival trickster. This is a vile slander spread by those who wish to destroy my reputation. But be warned, if I am to be cast down, I shall drag all my enemies with me. None shall escape!" The Old Lady was easily moved to rage, and to uttering dire threats about what was going to happen to those who opposed her.

It is true enough that Madame Blavatsky never claimed to be a magician, or to possess any magical secrets. At one point in her career she was a spiritualist, at another a religious leader. Always she claimed to be a seeker of occult truths. Yet she was firmly a part of nineteenth- and twentieth-century magic, and it was magic that bore the stamp of Madame's outsized personality.

Occultists and magicians have often claimed that they come from aristocratic stock. But H.P.B. really was an aristocrat. She could trace her ancestors back to a ninth-century grand duke of Moscow. Her father was an officer in the Russian army; her mother an unusually talented and lively woman who felt suffocated by the army camp existence she was forced to lead. She escaped as often as she could to the freer atmosphere of St. Petersburg, where she poured out her bitterness and disappointment in a series of novels. Helena and her mother were never very close, and her mother died while the child was still young. But it seems clear that it was from her mother that Helena inherited the unconventionality and cynicism that were to shape her later life.

Helena was born in 1831, and was reported to be a child whose imagination bordered on the hysterical. She spent most of her early years in army camps among peasant nurses and soldiers. It was a world where people wore charms to ward off the evil eye, and goblins and sinister spirits lurked around every dark corner. Helena could weave the peasant superstitions into wild fantasies with which she would terrify her companions. It was rumored that one was so frightened by Helena's stories that he was drowned while running away from what he believed to be evil spirits.

At the age of sixteen Helena impulsively married General Nikifor Blavatsky, a man some twenty years older than herself. The marriage was a farce and a disaster and the only thing Helena carried away from it was the general's name which she used for the rest of her life, though she seems to have married several other times. General Blavatsky and his wild child bride lived together for three months, when she abruptly returned to the home of her grandparents. Her grandparents tried to send her back to her father but Helena took up with the skipper of an English bark, and sailed for Constantinople.

For the next quarter of a century the career of Helena Petrovena Blavatsky is shrouded in mystery. An American traveler met her in Cairo in 1850. She was then working as a spirit medium and taking lessons from an Egyptian magician. Rumors also placed her in Paris, Constantinople, and London. Occasionally letters from Helena, or from different men claiming to be her husband, arrived in Russia and every few years Helena herself showed up.

The wandering years had changed her greatly. Though she was only thirty, a younger relative described her as being "old," fat, sloppy, and foulmouthed. The family tried to keep her hidden, but it was no use. Helena soon became a great favorite with younger people who were fascinated and amused by the various mediumistic feats she had picked up in her travels.

A key date in Madame Blavatsky's career was June, 1873. At that point she decided to cut her ties with the past and sailed for New York. It was a time when millions of immigrants were flooding into the United States, and Helena Blavatsky started her new life, as did many others, working in a sweatshop and living on New York's Lower East Side. But Madame was no ordinary immigrant, and she did not remain obscure for long.

Madame had come to America because America was the birthplace of spiritualism and she hoped to make her name and fortune as a spirit medium. At that time spiritualist circles were tremendously excited over the "manifestations" being produced at the farm of the Eddy brothers in rural Vermont. Madame traveled to Vermont to see what all the excitement was about. The Eddy brothers were crude tricksters, and their "manifestations" were dull. After Madame arrived the excitement picked up. She was never dull. Suddenly the farm seemed infested with spirits from Russia, Africa, India, and the plains of Asia. These spirits all spoke through the medium of Madame Helena Petrovena Blavatsky. It was at the Eddy farm that Madame first met Col. Henry S. Olcott, a prominent spiritualist who was to become her most faithful associate and follower.

Madame now began to move among the upper crust of American spiritualists, but spiritualism in the United States was in deep trouble. So many mediums had been exposed as out-and-out frauds, that even the most convinced spiritualists were badly shaken. Madame wrote to a Russian friend that she was willing to sell her soul for spiritualism, but no one was buying. Something new was needed.

Madame's associates were accustomed to receiving letters from the "spirits." But on March 9, 1875, Col. Olcott received a letter from a different source. The letter was written on green stationery in gold ink, and was signed Tuitit Bey, of the Brotherhood of Luxor. The letter urged Olcott to stick by Madame Blavatsky and she would lead him to "the Golden Gate of Truth."

Skeptics say the letter was written by Madame Blavatsky, and it was meant to stiffen Olcott's will. But she had linked up with one of the basic concepts of magic, that there exists somewhere a group of semidivine "masters" who control the "secrets of the ages." By choosing an Egyptian name for her masters, Madame had followed the ancient tradition that Egypt was the home of magic and mystery.

During this period Madame began evolving the set of beliefs that were to make her famous. She called the system theosophy, a word made from the Greek words meaning "knowledge of God." It is not possible to say just exactly what theosophy is, because the ideas kept changing under Madame's leadership, and later under the leadership of her successors. But like the ideas attributed to the Magi and the Rosicrucians, theosophy held that true knowledge of the universe was hidden from the world and could not be found in any of the accepted religions or sciences. Bits of the true knowledge had been revealed through the ages to various races that had preceded the human race on earth. The whole of the doctrine was now in the hands of the hidden masters, and only H.P.B. herself was in direct contact with them.

The Theosophical Society that was founded by Madame Blavatsky with Olcott's aid was to study this secret doctrine as revealed by the adepts through the agency of Madame Blavatsky.

Madame had taken a big step. She had abandoned spiritualism, though the messages from the adepts often sounded like the messages she had once received from the spirits. She might have taken the path of many other Western occultists and become involved in Hermetic theories and rituals. In fact, many of her followers were also interested in the Golden Dawn and vice versa. But as always Madame was an original.

She wrote a huge sprawling two-volume work called *Isis Unveiled.* The title indicates that she was still attracted by Egyptian mysteries. But a number of occultists had been traveling to the East, particularly to India, and returning with wondrous tales of the "miracles" performed by Hindu holy men. For some, India began to replace Egypt as the "Mother of Mysteries." Madame began incorporating some Hindu philosophy into her theories.

Then, impulsively, Madame decided to go to India, and she dragged a terrified Col. Olcott along with her. She said that she wished to learn more of "the secrets" from the holy men of India. But Madame had never been good at listening to others and in essence what she was trying to do was teach the Hindu religion to the Hindus. At first the Indian venture seemed absolutely mad, and Olcott told her so. But in the end she succeeded astonishly well. She began by winning converts from among the wealthy Hindus, then from among the British who ruled India. Hindu scholars and religious leaders were at first sympathetic to Madame Blavatsky, thinking that she was a Westerner sincerely interested in their religion. They soon discovered that H.P.B.'s theosophy and the Hindu religion were not the same, and they denounced her.

The Brotherhood of Luxor faded away in India. Soon H.P.B.'s followers began getting letters from a new source, "the Masters" or "the Mahatmas" who belonged to "the Great White Brotherhood." Like the old Egyptian Brotherhood, these new Masters were also semidivine, but they had Indian-sounding names, and were supposed to dwell in the far-off mountains of Tibet. Madame was the first to popularize Tibet as the home of all magic and mystery.

The Masters taught that all religions had certain truths, but that only theosophy possessed the ultimate truths and these would be revealed slowly. According to the Masters, the message theosophy had for humanity was, "There are three truths which are absolute and which cannot be lost, but yet may remain silent for lack of speech. The soul of man is immortal and its future is the future of the thing, whose growth and splendour has no limit. The principle which gives life dwells in us and without us, is undying and eternally beneficent, is not heard, or seen, or smelt, but is perceived by the man who desires perception. Each man is his own absolute lawgiver, the dispenser of glory or gloom to himself, decreer of his life, his reward, his punishment."

As you can see the meaning behind the words of Madame Blavatsky and other theosophists is difficult to understand. Enemies of theosophy say that there really is no meaning behind such words. But theosophists point out that all mystical, magical, and occult writings sound confusing and meaningless to outsiders. The inner meaning of the strange words can be grasped only after years of study and after receiving "illumination" from the powers beyond.

The Theosophical Society prospered in India, and its worldwide membership also grew. Madame bought a large estate near the village of Adyar, and entertained visitors from all over the world. People were most interested in improving their souls, or in spiritual enlightenment from theosophy. There was nothing in the doctrine that called for public miracles. Madame had frequently denounced any attempt to practice magic in any form. But she could never quite shake her addiction to cheap parlor tricks—"miracles" she called them. Today, some of those who believe in theosophy, and think that Madame was one of the greatest prophets in all history, are openly skeptical of her "miracles."

One of the cruder, but more effective devices was "the Shrine," a

Madame Blavatsky.

specially constructed wooden cabinet, placed in the Shrine Room next to Madame's own bedroom. Messages from the Mahatmas and gifts from other worlds appeared " miraculously" in the Shrine. Later investigators found that the Shrine was a trick box with trapdoors and sliding panels. Madame's accomplices hastily replastered the wall between the Shrine Room and her bedroom, before the investigators could examine it. But it is reasonable to suspect that this wall contained a hidden door.

Glimpses of the Masters in the flesh were also arranged. One of Madame's accomplices would make a robed dummy pop up from behind some trees or a clump of bushes.

Madame claimed that with the aid of the Masters anything, literally anything at all, was possible. But by making such a claim she was faced with the challenge of performing a real miracle—not something easily faked like having letters drop out of the sky or having objects appear in a trick box. The Masters were supposed to be able to travel anywhere in the world instantaneously. Someone proposed that as a test the Masters deliver a copy of the London *Times* to India on the same day that it was published, a physical impossibility in the nineteenth century. Madame, however, brushed aside the challenge. Of course, the Masters could do this if they wanted to, she replied, but the time was not right for such a miracle. It would send the vulgar masses flocking to theosophy before they were ready for it. Better the world be kept in doubt a bit longer. H.P.B. was not the first to use such an excuse and she would not be the last.

In 1884, H.P.B. was on a triumphal tour of Europe. She was welcomed by the best society in France, Germany, and England, but back at Adyar trouble was brewing. Dissension had broken out among the theosophists, and more ominous yet, an investigator from the influential Society for Psychical Research in London had arrived to check out Madame's claims. The investigator was a young man named Richard Hodgson who had originally been quite sympathetic to theosophy, but as he uncovered one shocking revelation after the other, he was moved to skepticism. Hodgson was aided by some of

Madame's disgruntled associates, as well as by numbers of absolutely sincere theosophists, who were quite sure there was nothing to hide. When the secret panels in the Shrine popped open, they could hardly believe their eyes.

Ultimately Hodgson summed up Madame Blavatsky with these words: "For our part, we regard her neither as the mouthpiece of hidden seers, nor as a mere vulgar adventuress; we think that she has achieved a title to permanent remembrance as one of the most accomplished, ingenious, and interesting imposters of history."

The revelations shook Madame Blavatsky's hold on the society that she had created. Many theosophists now regarded her as dangerously unreliable, and they tried to send her into retirement in Italy. But Madame refused to stay "retired" for long. Though she was quite ill, and had become so fat that she could barely walk, she began work on a new book, *The Secret Doctrine.* This book turned out to be even bigger and more popular than *Isis Unveiled.* Under the patronage of a couple of wealthy Englishmen, Madame moved back to London and set up her own branch of the Theosophical Society, to compete with the branch run from India. Poor Olcott, who had remained in India, pleaded that she was going to wreck the society with such tactics, but she ignored him, and he finally bowed to her wishes.

In 1889, Madame Blavatsky met and converted Annie Besant, a brilliant, successful, and restless woman who had been spokesman for a variety of radical causes. Two years later, on May 8, 1891, Madame Blavatsky died. The anniversary of her death is called White Lotus Day and is still observed by thousands of theosophists throughout the world. The lotus is a sacred flower in many parts of the Orient.

Many who think that Madame Blavatsky was a fraud, have to admit that there still was something almost supernatural about her, that she possessed some power the ordinary person does not have. Frank Podmore was a member of the British Society for Psychical Research, and he met H.P.B. in London. Podmore was a complete skeptic about theosophy, but he guessed that the Old Lady had the ability to hypnotize people, and perhaps to hypnotize herself into believing much of what she said. That is why she had been able to convince so many people of her special powers, even after she had been caught out in one trick after another. Perhaps this ability to make others believe is a trait shared by most of the great magicians in history.

After the Old Lady's death, the surviving theosophical leaders fought viciously for supremacy in the society. Mrs. Besant, because she was brighter and more energetic than the others, grabbed off the lion's share of the members. But she could never quite make the organization work the way the Old Lady had. Annie Besant lacked Madame Blavatsky's imagination. Mrs. Besant was assisted by a rather sinister character named Charles Leadbeater, a former minister with a habit of getting himself involved in nasty sexual scandals. On several occasions she tried to dump Leadbeater but found that she just couldn't get along without him. It was Leadbeater who dreamed up the weird rituals and ceremonies that theosophy came to rely upon.

The great achievement of theosophy was going to be to present the world with a new Messiah. To play this stellar role, Mrs. Besant and Leadbeater picked Jiddu Krishnamurti, a handsome Indian lad, who had been raised as a ward of the Theosophical Society and carefully groomed for his Messiahship. The fantastic scheme came to a humiliating conclusion in 1927, when Krishnamurti stood up before a great gathering of theosophists in the Netherlands and announced that he was no Messiah, and that all the theosophical rituals and dogmas were pointless. His only message to the world was that everybody must discover spiritual truths for himself. Preaching this simple doctrine, Krishnamurti retains a small, though influential, following today. But that was hardly what Annie Besant had in mind.

8
TODAY'S MAGICIANS

RIGHT NOW there are no really major magical stars like Aleister Crowley or Madame Blavatsky. This is in spite, or perhaps because, of the fact that there is a great revival of interest in magic and the occult. There are now so many magical types competing for public attention that it is hard to focus on a single individual.

Most of the magical claims today are centered in groups that say they are witchcraft cults or Devil-worshiping societies. Modern witches claim that they are practicing an ancient pre-Christian magical religion. According to these witches, they worship a horned god whom the Christians confused with Satan. Their rituals are supposed to help focus some sort of magical power—generally this power is assumed to be mental, spiritual, or "psychic."

The witches say that their cult has always been secret. Nonbelievers contend that no such cult ever existed. There was, of course, plenty of witchcraft in past ages, but no solid evidence that the witches were organized into any sort of cult. Witch was often just a general term for a person who tried to harm others by magic. From all available evidence the cult was invented in the late 1940's by Gerald B. Gardner, an English occultist who had once served as a customs official in Malaya. Gardner seems to have gotten most of his ideas from the theories of Margaret A. Murray, a British anthropologist, who tried to prove that there once had been a powerful underground witch cult or religion in Western Europe. Gardner contended that this underground cult still existed, and that he had been initiated into it. Most historians reject Professor Murray's theories and find Gardner's claims just plain silly. That didn't matter, because the idea captured the public's imagination. Witch cults suddenly began popping up all over England and the movement rapidly spread to America.

The most sensational thing about these modern witches is that they hold their meetings in the nude. This has given rise to stories about wild witchcraft orgies. Some of the stories may well be true, but in general, nudity is simply supposed to allow the magical power to radiate freely from the body without being blocked by clothes.

Witches, said Gardner, have been much maligned through history; they are not evil but good. He claimed that a group of English witches stopped Hitler from invading England in 1940, by a rite called The Great Cone of Power. Just exactly how this rite is performed was not revealed in any detail, but Gardner described the circumstances. The British witches were gathered together by a high priestess of witchcraft called Old Dorothy. "We were taken at night to a place in the Forest," wrote Gardner, "where the Great Circle was erected; and that was done which may not be done except in general emergency. The Great Cone of Power was raised and slowly directed in the general direction of Hitler. The command was given: 'You cannot cross the Sea. YOU CANNOT COME, YOU CANNOT COME.' Just as, we were told, was done to Napoleon when he had his army ready to invade England, and, as was done to the Spanish Armada, mighty forces were used, of which I may not speak. Now to do this means using one's life force; and many of us died a few days after we did this. My asthma, which I had never had since I went out

Gerald B. Gardner. Courtesy of the Witches Almanac, 1972 edition.

East, came back badly. We repeated the ritual four times; and the Elders said: 'We have stopped him. We must not kill too many of our people. Keep them until we need them.' "

A couple of individuals have managed to parlay popular interest in witchcraft into a considerable amount of personal notoriety. The most successful is Sybil Leek, a one-time English antique dealer, now living in Texas. She claimed to be queen of the British witches (a claim that enraged other British witches). According to Sybil Leek she belongs to the ancient witchcraft religion, but she seems far less interested in the ritual of witchcraft itself than was a person like Gerald Gardner. She is very involved in things like astrology, palm reading, and being a spirit medium. Sybil Leek says that all good witches must possess "psychic abilities" and therefore are successful at any kind of occult practice. But still, she has come a long way from traditional witchcraft.

Her younger and more attractive rival is Louise Heubner, from California. Miss Heubner hands out a lot of advice about how to improve your sex life through witchcraft. Though she advocates the use of the trappings associated with witchcraft, black candles, incantations, magic diagrams, and the like, she contends these are not absolutely necessary—they merely aid the witch in concentrating her "psychic energy."

Somewhat more ominous are those who declare themselves to be Satanists or Devil worshipers. Of these, Anton Szandŏr LaVey, head of the Church of Satan in San Francisco, has received the most attention. Whereas, at one time Devil worshipers were supposed to practice their abominable rites in the deepest secrecy, LaVey and his followers open their rites to the public, for the payment of a fee.

The ceremony begins in darkness, while Satanic hymns are played on the organ. Candles are lit revealing men wearing black robes and pointed hoods. The women in the ceremony wear black robes without hoods. LaVey himself wears a black cape and a skullcap with horns. He normally shaves his head and sports a pointed beard.

In this Satanic ceremony a nude female is stretched out upon the altar. LaVey takes a sword and offers up various invocations to Satan. The officiating priest then takes a chalice, which may be filled with any liquid from lemonade to whisky, and makes a symbolic offering to Satan, after which the chalice is placed upon the nude girl, where it remains for the rest of the service.

With these opening ceremonies out of the way members of the congregation come forward into the circle of hooded priests, and are asked what they desire. This can be money, power, love, revenge—anything at all. The priest touches the member with his sword and asks the congregation to focus all their emotional power on the request that has been made. After each member of the congregation has gone through this process the proceedings are brought to a close.

Much of this, and other Satanic rituals practiced by LaVey and his followers, comes from the writings of Aleister Crowley, or from the practices attributed to Devil worshipers of past ages. But there is one great difference, LaVey does not believe in magic, or in Satan either. His philosophy is grounded in the theory that man is a selfish and brutal creature, and that Christianity and the other religions that proclaim the potential goodness of men are hypocritical. In his *Satanic Bible* LaVey inverts Christian doctrine, "Blessed are the strong, for they shall possess the earth." "If a man smite you on one cheek, SMASH him on the other." LaVey and his followers profess to look down upon anyone who really believes in the supernatural.

But doctrines, such as those of Anton Szandŏr LaVey, present a paradox. There is nothing particularly new or startling about saying that man is selfish and brutal and should act accordingly. What really attracts people is all the magical window dressing which is supposed to be only incidental. Why use it at all? LaVey says that the rituals help to focus the emotional powers within each individual. His magic is entirely psychological. But this belief is not very far from many traditional magical theories which regard the ritual and magical implements as mere aids, and say that the real secret of magic lies within the individual.

Magic of this sort can present a real danger to those who become too deeply involved in it. Even in America today there are cases where persons who believed they were being hexed became ill, died, or have killed themselves. Others have committed murder in the belief that they were performing some sort of magical ritual. But the percentage of those who have become dangerously involved in magic and the occult is tiny. Such individuals are generally deeply disturbed anyway and their beliefs in magic were rarely the cause for their violent acts.

Drugs present a more serious problem. Historically there has been an association between magic and drugs. It was the cunning man or woman who dispensed the herbal medicine. Some of those herbs had hallucination-producing or consciousness-altering effects. Many of the marvelous magical conjurations were the products of drugged fantasies. Modern occultists were often heavy drug users. Crowley was famous for his addiction, and Madame Blavatsky was said to be a regular user of hashish. In modern magical doctrine the line between physical and emotional reality is blurred. If, as some believe, the aim of modern magic is changing the state of consciousness, then drugs may be at the very core of the modern magical experience.

But for most of us magic is just a diversion, a stimulating brush with the arcane and the exotic. So long as it remains that way, all the posturing and chanting, all fantastic theories and outlandish costumes, can be fun to observe.

INDEX